I0439218

The Tale of Religious Wars and Economic Woes

Author: Shabbir H M Tankiwala

Copyright @ 2016   Author All Rights Reserved

Man has/have created Religion, Religion has not created man. Religion is a man-made device designed to focus people's attention and energy on a single unchanging and uncompromising supreme being.

Religions survives because of People, but, People do not survive because of religions.

Who created whom? Humans created God a figment of our imagination or god created human beings.

People throughout history have created a god to meet their own needs and circumstances. But, the REAL God of the Universe cannot be the creation of mere man's logic and mental comprehension.

We are not "God," but our desire to be such takes us to madness.

Majority among us (humans) waste invaluable time of ours in our life time, thinking about God, talking about God, discussing about God, promoting god, defending god, gosh' so much god, most of the people we talk too, they use the word "**God**" as many time as they can possibly use during the course of the conversation, these devout religious people start conversation with the name of "God" and ends the conversation with the name of "God." Around the world many people spend unprecedented amount of their time in their life-time "thinking, talking, reading and understanding of or about <u>God</u>," so much time of theirs in their life-time is invested in God that they fail to understand their own-selves, such people who devout lot of their time and energy for religious purpose and in thinking and talking about god, apparently have less confidence in themselves and it invariably makes them less productive.

The power to manipulate beliefs is all that matters most, because we humans live with beliefs and it is always easy to manipulate beliefs.

People around the World become victim of propaganda, it is because most of the people are **NOT** Intellectually Competent.

Uncertain times are becoming even more uncertain, these are challenging moments for the entire humanity, sort out one problem and another problem rushes in, too many challenges but too few resources available to solve ever existing difficult problems and for dealing with incredibly difficult challenges.

Far too many challenges before us, so many problems, despite so many remarkably intelligent and well-judging minds, yet difficult to find solutions for most of the problems we humans are burdened with.

Social problems, healthcare related problems, widespread religious and racial discrimination, ecological imbalance and climatic problems, demographic problems, so many problems and challenges, but, who are responsible for all these excruciating problems?

Rising religious intolerance and hatred crimes, steady increase in domestic violence and workplace violence, increased cases of sexual harassments, forced marriages, forced prostitutions and gruesome incidents of honour killings, women and children particularly vulnerable.

Crisis is either created by man or crisis is created by nature.

The problems with problem is that one problem creates many more problems

Racial, cultural and religious prejudice, worst is religious prejudice, we humans for generations have been a divided lot, we people, living and surviving in deeply polarized world, because of unequal distribution of resources our society with extensive inequality is brutally polarized on cultural and religious line.

People like to do favours for person or persons belonging to their own religious sect or ethnic and religious community, as callous as they can be, when it comes to making choices, preferential treatment is given to person or persons belonging to their own religious or ethnic community, great people never hesitate a bit to ensure they render productive help and support to person of their own community, even if that person is less deserving and have insignificant talent and skills, yet they'll provide that person an opportunity and overlook more deserving candidates, therefore, this is how, many talented and deserving folks lose out on jobs and professional opportunities, and, instead, inept and undeserving candidates gets selected, this is, why? We see many nonsense people achieve great success in life and honest people career and life is destroyed.

People's integrity is more with the religion they follow and Not with Humanity.

People are liked or disliked, Not for, "What they are," But for, "Who they are."

Too many things to worry about, new age modern technology creating few jobs and professional opportunities, but, destroying more jobs, unemployment is a problem but underemployment is even bigger problem, because around the world many <u>high-performers and degree holders</u> are unable to find suitable jobs or professional opportunities matching their skills hence compel to do **low-paying and low-skill** job or work. These are without any doubt most horrendously difficult times for the entire humanity.

What is more dangerous? And, what is it that is harming humanity the most in 21st century? What this world be like when we enter the 22nd century? These are some of the most pressing questions and concerns, rise in "extremism, terrorism and religious and sectarian conflicts and violence, even more chaotic is > deteriorating natural environment, climatic problems, unpredictable weather," difficult to find quick solutions, it's a fluid situation.

Terrorism, Islamic fundamentalism (jihadi army) or Economic problems, combination of all three factors are responsible for brutally destroying this wonderful <u>Planet</u> of ours **the Earth**. Irresponsibly planned "flawed and faulty economic and international trade policies are having profound and devastating effect and is causing unprecedented harm and damage to natural environment and ecosystem which causes brutal climatic problems," therefore unfounded and irrational beliefs of many that it is terrorism that is menacing and is harming humanity, well, think again, more people around the world are dying or experiencing many types of other excruciating problems all because of more frequent natural disasters.

Hundreds of millions of people around the world are internally displaced, homeless and have lost their source of income because of weather related problems, arable and fertile farmlands have become arid and infertile, rivers and lakes are drying up, extremely treacherous heat, floods and flash floods, summer are getting more warmer and winters are getting less chilly.

If we talk and discuss about 21st century challenges, and, what will be the future outlook of global economic and politics? There are political risk, economic risk, deteriorating ecological system, unable to solve ever increasing <u>environmental</u> and <u>climatic problems</u>, all because of growing religious intolerance and sharp increase in incidents of hate crimes. <u>Capitalists economic system</u> "economic policies are planned and implemented to benefit tiny world's population for those who are Rich, influential and power individual people and for the large corporate houses and industries," therefore, small percentage or so to say just 2% of global population is/are immensely benefiting from **Capital-markets** friendly liberal economic policies, but, remaining population of the world is suffering intolerable level of economic hardship, dwindling annual income, higher inflation, ever so rising cost of living, all these factors makes it increasingly difficult for ordinary citizens of the world to sustain themselves and survive.

For large majority of world's population there is no access to clean water or functional toilets, structural discrimination and infrastructure deficiency, especially hurts women the most as they (female-gender) are unable to maintain high quality hygiene, for average people on the street, for them it is difficult to afford food and unable to get better healthcare facilities.

Who is responsible for plight of large majority of world's population? **People themselves**, overwhelming majority of world's population firmly believes that some sort of divine intervention will solve their problems and divine blessings will bring peace, prosperity and happiness in their life.

So much misleading information with regards to gods and goddesses, disinformation campaign by vested interest that **saints** and **angels** will perform miracles and will defeat the evil and cure diseases and will help bring incredible economic gain to you, people around the world waste enormously valuable time of their own practicing religious rituals and reading the so-called religious holy books, which are nothing but full of contradictions, unscientific narratives, vague and some laughable stories of divine healing super-natural power of god and falsely described and highly exaggerated events.

Do we really need religion/religions? Can't we humans survive without a religion? What are religions there for? Each damn religion preaches that their religion is the most authentic religion and best way to move closer to seek "Divine Blessings," they (priests and clerics) will always say to their followers that ours is the best religion and all other religions and religious beliefs are blunt, every religion claims that their religion is best and more holy compare to every other religions, such perception and conviction, well, I would say, it is indeed very scary, each people think their religion is superior than every other religions, it is because generation after generation parents and grandparents indoctrinates the minds of their children with religious thoughts and preaches them about supernatural power that their alleged God or Prophet possesses, it is so because people are not ready to open their mind and try to establish the truth "if at all there exist any element such as "God." Religion is one of the most sensitive issues and, although every religion encourages the idea of peace and tolerance, almost no one remains in peace or tolerates anything when it comes to their religion. History is full of **religious wars** and some of them have continued for years and killed **many**.

To my mind, Religion is a tool to manipulate mankind, religion and religious beliefs takes over full control over the minds of great masses.

Various religious institutions uses brainwashing, mind control, oppression, false teaching, guilt, shame, peer pressure and other bondage techniques to control members of their Sect and religious community, the underlying agenda of religious institution is desire to obtain power control and money.

When we talk of money, "**Power of money**" is perhaps the most powerful strength an individual or a country or religious sect can possess, Power of money helps gain Political power vice a versa Political power helps obtain Power of money, and if a person can obtain both the powers (economic and political) that person is arguably the most fortunate person.

Be it economic or political "**power**" is all about numbers, if a particular ethnic group or religious community is largest or second largest denomination in the country, if your religious community has the largest population in the country you live in, than, there are strong chances that a person from your community will control the political & economic system hence will become leader and rule the country, for example; if head-of-state or ruler of the country belongs to Sunni Muslim community than he/she will overwhelmingly work for the causes of Sunni Muslim population and demographics, similarly if the ruler is Roman catholic he/she will help the Roman catholic population of that country, so overtly or more subtly, it has been observed that in each country ruling political class always have bias feelings and attitude, they favour particular group of people mostly belonging to their own religious sect or community and ignores or in some case even discriminates another group/groups who are not their supporters or considered to be belonging to rival ethnic or religious communities.

Since Christianity with all its denomination (for example: Roman catholic, Anglicanism, Protestants and Eastern-orthodox Christians, etc) is largest population in the world, according to some estimate suggests as of 2015 Christian population is 2.4 billion, therefore not surprising that majority of world's nations and countries are ruled and governed by Christians. And now Islam have 2nd largest population in the world, as of 2015 Muslim population again with all its denomination (for eg: Sunnis, Shiites, and other sub-caste and communities) are

1.7 billion, therefore again no surprise that after Christianity other majority of world's nations and countries are controlled and ruled by Muslim rulers.

What worries not only Christianity but other major religious communities such as Judaism, Hindus and Buddhists or even the non-believers atheists is rapid rise in Islamic population, yes, Islam is world's fastest growing religion, Islamist population is increasing at phenomenal pace, and threatening to become world's largest religion outstripping <u>Christianity</u>, unless something dramatically different happens or else by the year 2050 **Islam** will become world's largest religion, for the past Two thousand years or more Christianity has/have vehemently dominated global economics and politics, but today it concerns Christian institutions that sharp rise in Muslim population will ultimately decimate Christianity's control and power in world's economic and politics and Islamists will make Christians second class citizens. Unprecedented power of Islam will potentially increase globally the risk of more religious wars, and precipitate hatred crimes on the streets and at workplace.

Anyone interested in knowing, what is/are the reason for such spectacular rise in Muslim population worldwide? Muslim population growing at 5 to 6% annually, whereas every other religious communities including Christianity, Hindus and Buddhists population growing insignificantly at just 1% or at best 1½% annually, in fact in some countries non-Muslim population is sharply declining, due to economic uncertainty and environmental problems, many young girls and women from non-Muslim religious communities are deferring marriage plan and even if married due to higher cost of living and rising expenses most married females are delaying pregnancy for indefinite period of time, also it has been noticed "most of the non-Muslim married couples are reluctant to have more than one child."

So it is creating serious demographic problems around the world for non-Muslim religious communities or those who are atheists unbelievers, as they all practice strict family planning and birth control, whereas in sharp contrast unconcerned about economic hardship, unperturbed about any kind of social consequences the Islamic folks believe in enjoying sex without any contraception, Muslim religious hierarchy and community leaders as well the politicians openly encourage Muslim folks to have as many offspring as possible, Islamic institutions and Muslim leaders openly in public speaks favouring increasing Islamic population advises Muslim women not to remain single and once married should give birth to at least 3 children, yes its true, Muslim clerics call for each Muslim women to have at least 3 kids if not more, Islam mantra is "more the better," Islam needs higher population of Muslims because only with higher number of followers of Islam, that'll actually help in establishing **Islamic caliphate** (Islamic rule) the world over, Islam's more open agenda is to conquer the world, and for that it needs a big army, people who are ready to sacrifice their lives for the cause of Islam.

Since Islam as a religion is growing at fast pace and strengthening its bases, so people around the world discusses lot more about Islam, Islamic motives and actions are more seriously scrutinized, on the flip side there are serious differences within Islam, internal rift due to sectarian and ideological divide therefore Islamic sectarian conflicts and civil wars in many Muslim dominated countries and Islamic internal problems and high level of corruption is/are creating problems for entire world's population, this planet earth is becoming increasingly dangerous place to live and to survive, terrorism, religious wars and more often brutal natural disasters all combination of reasons makes this world more unsafe.

Skin colour prejudice, linguistic chauvinism, but religious prejudice is main reason behind ever so continuing religious wars, first revolution in human history it seems happened <u>Twelve thousand years ago</u> was **Agriculture revolution**, which changed the dynamics of humanity, agriculture revolution, growing food grains and vegetables for human consumption helped in rapid progress and development of humanity, rapid progress and development also increased pressure on we humans to perform and to become more productive, in an effort to be competitive and to improve living standards further and to become more productive, we humans became vehemently greedy, and our greed is what comprehensively divided us.

we humans formed several groups and divided ourselves in many different groups, and each group of people considered a person or persons from another group and groups as outsiders and started treating them as their rivals, such formed social system caused structural divisions, based on colour of their skin or language they speak, and this is what we call it as **caste or community system**, boundaries were drawn, so, "**one world, one language, one currency, one country system was**

broken" because of sharp difference among humans, people started forming groups and therefore society was divided, this is perhaps how various different nations and countries came into existence, some people were allowed entry while others were fiercely restricted from entering territory, villages and cities were/are reserved to be occupied by people belonging to particular racial or community group, "(*so this is why, in modern times, we need to have passport and need to obtain visa so that we can travel to another country and if visa is not provided we can't legally travel to that particular country*)."

Agriculture revolution helped establish Family System, men and women started valuing their intimate relationship, because men were worried, they wanted to ensure whether or not certain children are theirs biologically, because they wanted to leave their accumulated wealth and property to their own biological child, women and men started making very clear connection between sexual behaviour and birth. The advent of agriculture changed everything about human society, from sexuality to politics to economics to health to diet to exercise patterns to work-versus-rest patterns. It introduced the notion of property into sexuality. Property wasn't a very important consideration when people were living in small, foraging groups where most things were shared, including food, childcare, shelter and defence. So, before agriculture, sex was relatively promiscuous, and paternity was not a concern, in a similar way to the mating system of Bonobos. Sexual interactions strengthened the bond of trust in the groups; far from causing jealousy, social equilibrium and reciprocal obligation was strengthened by playful sexual interactions. People of particular community or skin colour started claiming full control and ownership of available resources hidden under the surface such as mineral mines, oil and gas, or the fertile land.

Various social groups based on their skin colour or linguistic affiliation in early primitive era formed caste and community system, these social groups were further upgraded to **Religion status**, so this is how various Religions came into effect, **religion system** was perhaps created so that people or to say followers of that particular religion will remain united and unitedly will face challenges if any, but as it is evident that religion system has comprehensively failed itself, there is brutal division in almost every major or minor religion, Christianity is divided into many denomination and factions, prominent among them are "Roman catholic, Protestants, Anglicanism, Eastern-orthodox Christians, Coptic Christians and so many more smaller denominations," similarly **Islam** is savagely divided religion, two prominent faction of Islam are <u>Shiite</u> and <u>Sunni</u> but these two communities as well have many more sub-community and offshoots, similarly **Paganism** is ancestor religion of entire humanity, Paganism as well is/was divided unit, and various pagan religious groups and community "kings and queens, alleged gods and goddesses" kept fighting among themselves.

So, disunity and conflict of interest creates division, and divisions further divides the society, when groups of people owing allegiance to rival religion or denomination of same religious sect thinks, it would be fair to fight physical wars in open battle field, consider other group of people from different religious community as your enemy and snatch wealth from them.

So religious wars are fought when there is discontent and strong disagreement over issues, no dialogue and no amicable solution found between governments of countries ruled by rival religious sect or religious communities > for example; "India is majority Hindu country and its neighbour Pakistan is Islamic nation, similarly Saudi Arabia and Turkey are Sunni-Muslim dominated countries and their neighbours Iran and Iraq are Shia majority nations," most likely and common cause of problems for religious wars and civil wars are disagreement and disputes over "sharing of wealth, water resources or other resources like minerals or usage of land for agriculture or transportation purpose,"

In recorded history most ferocious and brutal wars are fought between denominations of same religious communities, Roman catholic have fought bitter bloody wars with Protestants, similarly in Judaism various faction have serious differences over religious issues, and in Islam the rival faction Shias and Sunnis have been fighting ferocious battles ever since they've come into existence.

After the end of 1st and 2nd world wars, most of religious wars fought in many different countries have some kind of Muslim involvement.

Talking about religious intolerance and religious wars, **Sudan** was once a prominent African country, Sudanese experienced nearly 4 to 5 decades long (between 1955 till 2005) bloodiest civil war, in united <u>Sudan</u> the northern part of country had near total Sunni-Muslim population and southern region of Sudan had majority Christian population, Muslims in majority wanted to have total Sharia Law (Islamic religious law) enforce all over the country and Muslims trying their best to restrict Christianity from freely practising their faith, also other issues that created problems between Christians and Muslims was, that, while northern region of Sudan has rich fertile land suitable for agriculture, the southern region of country has large reserves of **petroleum oil**, Muslims also wanted to have control over oil reserves, so for combination of reasons both "Islamic jihadi army and Christian militia and rebels" fought fierce battle, it has been reported that nearly 2 million people belonging to both religious community were killed and millions more displaced and suffered fatal injuries, finally solution was found when Sudan was divided into two countries, Muslims retaining its control and rule over northern part of Sudan and **south-Sudan** a land-lock country in north-eastern Africa gained its independence from Sudan in 2011 and became a new country ruled by Christians.

Iran and **Iraq** war fought between 1980 to 1988, was by no mean an ordinary political war between two neighbouring countries, it was a war between two hostile denomination of Islam, it was war between two diverse ideology of same religion fiercely oppose to each other, at that time majority Shiite country Iraq was ruled by a Sunni tyrant dictator <u>Saddam Hussein</u>, also worth noting that Saddam in 1980s was staunch western ally, hence was fully backed by fellow Sunni Arab countries and U.S.A., Saddam for no apparent reason he forcefully attacked Iran, of course Iran retaliated with vengeance, Iran – Iraq conflict was bloodiest religious war, the two denomination of Islam Shiite and Sunni army fighting relentlessly and resolutely to destroy each other.

The then Iraqi Sunni dictator <u>Saddam Hussein</u> on 16th-March-1988 ordered his army to use lethal **chemical weapons** on minority Kurdish community in northern Iraqi village of **Halabja** nearly 4000 Kurdish community people were inhumanly killed, and another 5 to 7 thousand were critically injured, but, since Saddam at that time was rich and resourceful and was blue-eyed boy of the western countries, hence there was lukewarm response from world's powerful countries for such a cruel crime that Saddam and his army had committed, only mild condemnation, leading politicians maintained stoic silence.

In the 1990s **Bosnian war** was one of the deadliest and bloodiest religious war ever fought in Europe, Bosnian Serb forces and militants butchered the mainly Albanian Muslims, Bosnia war is infamous for war crimes that were committed during conflict, Bosnian Serb army had allegedly used unique and exclusive methods to torture their enemy, and it were mainly the Muslims who became victims of heinous war crimes, sexual and other form of violence and **rape as weapon of war**, the reported cases of Bosnian war crimes against humanity that will profoundly shame entire humanity.

Jews in Europe were subjected to progressively harsh persecution that ultimately led to the murder of 6,000,000 Jews. Jews were the victims of Germany's deliberate and systematic attempt to annihilate the entire Jewish population of Europe, the Holocaust known as the Final Solution, which called for the systematic extermination of all Jews and the other scapegoats. It is goal of the Christians to expunge the Jewish population from the world and not the principle objective of Islam alone.

Armenian genocide also known as **Armenian holocaust**, incontrovertible evidence proves that Ottoman Turks Islamic army carried out genocide against Armenians, killings and massacres of innocent unarmed Armenian people, in 1915 Ottoman authorities set plan in motion to expel Armenians who were living in Ottoman empire territory, it was ethnic cleansing, estimate suggest 1.5 million Armenians were brutally killed.

Article title "**The first genocide of 20ᵗʰ century happened in Namibia**" describes "Turks carried out genocide against the Armenians in 1915. But the oft-repeated assertion that it was the first genocide of the 20th century is wrong: it was the attempted annihilation of the Herero by the Germans in South-West Africa (present-day Namibia) from 1904 to 1907.

The language, methods, and scale of the Herero genocide remain shocking even in the aftermath of the horrors of the Holocaust. In their quest to occupy and exploit the territory of the pastoralist Herero, the German colonizers recruited a mercenary army led by Lt. Gen. Lothar von Trotha. The Vernichtungsbefehl ("Destruction Order") he issued was terrifyingly clear: "Within the German borders, every Herero, whether armed or unarmed, with or without cattle, shall be shot."

The genocide culminated in the infamous "march into death" of Herero who were forced into the Omaheke Desert. The Germans sealed the perimeter with guard towers, poisoned water sources, and then bayoneted to death Herero who attempted to escape dehydration. An official history of the German General Staff compiled after the genocide rightly concluded: "The arid Omaheke was to complete what the German army had begun: the annihilation of the Herero people." Those who survived the desert were sent to concentration camps where captured Herero soldiers, along with women and children, were forced to work. Women boiled and scraped the skin off the heads of Herero who had been killed. Those skulls were then shipped off to Germany for museum displays and eugenics research.

Recent articles highlight that Hitler, while planning the Final Solution, dismissively remarked "Who remembers the Armenian genocide?" Indeed, even less known was (and remains) the Herero genocide which has many parallels with the Holocaust: the destruction order, the concentration camps, the forced labour. The so-called scientific research by German geneticist Eugen Fischer, who argued that mixed-race children in South-West Africa were inferior to the offspring of German parents, was cited in Hitler's *Mein Kampf*."..............

Saudi Arabia is a wealthy nation, the largest petroleum oil producing and exporting country in the world, Saudi is also largest arms and defence equipment importing country in the world, Saudi Arabia dominant Sunni nation following **Wahhabi-Islam**, Saudi Arabia attacked its impoverish neighbouring country "**Yemen**," Yemen is arguably the poorest country in the world, Saudi army committed genocide inside Yemen, specifically targeting cities and villages in Yemen which are dominated by its rival Shia community population, between 2015 &16, Saudi Airforce bombarded Houthi Shiite dominated towns in Yemen, not even sparing innocent civilian population, mercilessly killing young children and women, it has been reported at least 8000 people mostly civilians were killed in Saudi Airstrikes, and thousands more suffered brutal wounds and injuries, besides massive loss and damage to properties, Saudi army used same **weapons** that it purchased from western countries like France, Britain and America, while Saudi armed forces inhumanly kept attacking desperately poor "Shiite Houthi" population inside Yemen, the western governments otherwise big advocates of human rights and civil rights maintained stoic silence, did nothing to stop and to prevent Saudi government from attacking and killing the hapless Shiite Muslim Yemeni population.

Injustice invariably leads to rebellion and retaliation, Jewish and Muslim religious wars over the control of Israeli territory, while Muslim say *"the land is not Israel but Palestine, and Israel is rightfully land of Islamists and Jewish have illegally captured their land and made Muslims homeless in their own country,"* but, Jewish community strongly oppose Islamic claim, says, Israel is and always been Jewish territory, cites historic proof from biblical era, Israel was land of Hebrew people, so, allegation and counter allegation, each side not willing to relent hence no peaceful solution found, therefore west-bank and Gaza strip has become a battle ground, **Palestine liberation force** and more militant terror organization **Hamas** fighting against official Israeli army, injustice breeds intolerance and once religious wars starts than it goes on and on for protracted period of time. That's exactly what is happening between two Abrahamic religion **Judaism** and **Islam**, no end in hostility, since 1950s until 2015 thousands of people from both community have lost their life, Islamic terrorists seeking revenge are targeting Jewish population all over the world, attacking and killing Jewish people and desecrating Jewish holy places of worship.

While Jewish and Muslim religious wars continues and no amicable solution being worked out, equally brutal are religious wars within the same religion and sectarian strife between two denomination of Islam the **Shias** and **Sunnis** continues because they as well are unable to find amicable solutions to solve millennium old religious problems and sharp differences over religious issues, the first major confrontation between Shiite and Sunni was on 10th- October-680 AD, on this day Sunni jihadi army slaughtered revered Shia Imam '**Imam Hussein**' in battle of Karbala present day in Iraq, in battle of Karbala Sunni army had mercilessly killed Imam Hussein and more than 70 of his supporters which included his family members, relatives and sympathizers who fought against Sunni army and sacrificed their life, so, ever since 7th century the two main faction of Islam the Shiite and Sunni have never shared cordial relation with each other.

It is goal of Sunnis to wipe out Shia Islam by all means possible, in 21st century, Shia army and militias are fighting fierce battle against formidable Sunni jihadists, the Saudis, Kuwaitis and Qataris generously funding the jihadists to fight multiple battles against Iranian backed Shiite army at multiple locations in west-Asia, Islamic sectarian conflict between Shia and Sunni in "Lebanon, Syria, Iraq and Yemen," continues, between 2011 and 2016 more than million people killed or wounded, millions of people internally displaced, homeless and jobless. Sunni dominated countries such as "Turkey, Saudi Arabia, Kuwait and UAE" are staunch western allies, therefore it is alleged many Sunni jihadists subtly and indirectly receives unflinching support from western countries, strange but not surprising many Sunni jihadi when critically injured or wounded fighting inhuman jihad (Islamic holy-war) inside Syria or even in Iraq receives medical treatments -- guess; 'where?' nowhere else but in Israeli hospitals, yes, it has been reported that Jewish doctors are rendering best quality medical treatment to many of the wounded Jihadis. Secret nexus between Sunni Arab states and Jewish state Israel.

Religious wars within same religion are not uncommon, similarly like Shiite and Sunni in Islam, in Christianity the two major denomination **Roman catholic** and **Protestants** have fought many wars, in Ireland or in France or during Roman empire in Rome there is sordid history of many wars fought between various Christian factions, in Buddhist or among Hindus, in India caste system where upper caste Hindus discriminates lower caste Hindus, upper caste Hindu landlords brutally harass lower caste Hindus also rape and worst still in extreme cases they **parade naked** low-caste Hindu women.

India has become hotbed for religious riots between Hindus and Muslims, legendary Greek king **Alexander** the Great had once famously said "**India is a -- Golden Sparrow,**" however he met little success in conquering India, but Britishers and Moghuls (Muslim kings from Persia and Arabia) greatly succeeded in conquering India, India was one of the first country in the world to transition from barter system to money based trade system along with the Greeks, also worth noting is that undivided India, once Pakistan and Bangladesh were both very much an integral part of India until the partition in 1947, other fact is that <u>India</u> was and still is deeply socio-culturally and religiously polarized nation.

Merchants and traders from Great Britain succeeded in establishing British Raj (Rule) in Indian and kings and queens of England ruled India for nearly 150 years, British merchants and traders travelled all their way from England to India, initially their purpose was to do trade and conquering India was not on their agenda, but to trade in agri-commodities and for slave trade, compare to any other countries India had big population and therefore had large percentage of skilled and semi-skilled workforce and Britishers badly and desperately needed manpower especially trained agriculture farm labourers and construction workers to work on construction cities and develop many of their colonies or British ruled countries scattered around the world, and India was the best place to source labour, tens of thousands of Indian men and women were relocated to many different countries under British rule to work as farm cultivator, especially in sugar farming and hard labourers to work on civil engineering projects, besides to power the growth of industries in Britain, Spices, jute and cotton such agri-commodities were exported from India to UK, but while trading with India, the British also explored India and studied the basic socio-cultural and economic system of the country, when they found India is socio-culturally brutally divided, many different caste and religion do not get along well and do not trust each other, that's when British merchants did a rethink, and started working on the plan to exploit the situation and best strategy was *divided and rule*.

Sharp differences between Hindus and Muslims, plus caste system in Hinduism, Hindus divided between upper caste and lower-caste, the more influential upper-caste Hindus for generations suppressing and treating lower-caste Hindus like dogs and cats, when British were convince that India's social and economic system is feeble and fragmented and people are vulnerable, the astute British merchants exploited the situation to their advantage, the British smartly targeted the suppressed and weaker section of the Indian society, and tempted them to join British army, so sometime around late 18th century and early 19th century the British used Indian money and Indian citizens to fight against fellow Indians, yes, to fight and to conquer India almost 90% of soldiers in British army were Indians, and British army than fought wars against the rulers who were from both Muslim and Hindu communities of many small and big kingdoms inside India, and that's how the British controlled trading company **"The East India Company"** succeeded in establishing British Raj (rule), and later in 1858 till 1947 India was officially ruled by official government of Great-Britain, England's **Queen Victoria** was proclaimed Empress of India in 1876.

Not just **British rule** was establish in India, but Christian missionaries and representatives from several European churches as well have exploited the lower-caste Hindus, and allegedly have been working to convert the idolaters in India, particularly targeting the weaker and deprived section of the society, offering them food, fruits and cakes, giving them admission in missionaries run schools, brainwashing and systematically forcing them by bribing, torture, deceit and blackmailing to convert to Christianity. Both the main Abrahamic religion Christianity and Islam have used fraudulent and oppressive methods to tarnish paganism and to convert Pagans the believers of multiple gods and goddesses and worshipers of nature in India

Religious tensions have always remain high in India, between Hindus and Christians, but more profound is hostility between Hindus and Muslims, large and resourceful country India was divided when Islamists selfishly demanded either hand us complete rule of India or a large piece of Indian land and territory be given to Muslims, between 1920 and 1950 was devastatingly stressful period for Indians, frequent communal violence and riots, thousands of people were killed, ultimately after unprecedented violence and massacres and tough negotiations between Hindu and Muslim religious and political leaders the country was finally divided on communal lines, the Muslim nation **Pakistan** was created.

Partitioning and dividing India in 1947, has not helped matters, tensions and ill-feelings between both the dominant communities "Hindus and Muslims" persist, hatred crimes have increased, India and Pakistan have fought several wars, situation on Indo-Pak border is always tense and grim, frequent violence and riots between Hindus and Muslims in many different Indian towns and cities, in India the minority Muslims accuses the majority Hindus of discrimination and depriving them of jobs and business opportunities, while in Pakistan the Muslims treats small minority Christian and Hindu population not even as 2nd class but renders 3rd class treatment to them, inside Pakistan minority Hindus and Christians are treated like 3rd class citizens, often abused and physically tortured besides young women and girls sexually exploited.

Once an integral part of undivided "India," than was recognized and east-Pakistan, than it fought and gained freedom and became independent country, here I'm talking about **Bangladesh**, the economic and social crisis in Arabian and African Muslim dominated countries, rise in Islamic jihadists activities and terrorism, and unrelenting Islamic religious wars that started in year 2011 have seriously impacted Bangladesh, otherwise a country of art loving people, Bangladesh as well have been experiencing religious intolerance and rise in communal violence, the jihadists owing allegiance to either ISIS or Al Qaeda, have tear the Bangladesh social fabric into pieces, the Islamists jihadi elements increasingly terrorizing the liberal and secular activists, killing the secular minded "Artists, blog writers and thinkers," tearing the gays and homosexuals into pieces, the Sunni-jihadists more often assaults and kills the minority Christians and Hindus, especially hitting hard to the religious priests and desecrating the religious temples.

Some scholars have said "Religion holds back progress," religious intolerance is global phenomenon, Europe has experienced many religious wars, here are Excerpts from **"European wars of Religions'** sourced from >Wikipedia," "The **European Wars of Religion** were a series of religious wars waged in Europe from ca. 1524 to 1648, following the onset of the **Protestant Reformation** in Central & Western and Northern Europe. Although sometimes unconnected, all of these wars were strongly influenced by the religious change of the period, and the conflict and rivalry that it produced. This is not to say that the combatants can be neatly categorized by religion or were divided by their religion alone, as this was often not the case.

The first large-scale violence was engendered by the more radical of Luther's followers, who wished to extend wholesale reform of the Church to a similar wholesale reform of society in general. This was a step which the princes who supported Luther were in no way willing to countenance. The German Peasants' War of 1524/1525 was a popular revolt inspired by the teachings of the radical reformers. It consisted of a series of economic as well as religious revolts by <u>peasants</u>, townsfolk and <u>nobles</u>. The conflict took place mostly in southern, western and central areas of modern Germany but also affected areas in neighboring modern Switzerland and Austria. At its height, in the spring and summer of 1525, it involved an estimated 300,000 peasant insurgents. Contemporary estimates put the dead at 100,000. It was Europe's largest and most widespread popular uprising before the 1789 <u>French Revolution</u>.

Because of their revolutionary political ideas, radical reformers like Thomas Müntzer were compelled to leave the Lutheran cities of North Germany in the early 1520s. They spread their revolutionary religious and political doctrines into the countryside of Bohemia, Southern Germany, and Switzerland. Starting as a revolt against feudal oppression, the peasants' uprising became a war against all constituted authorities, and an attempt to establish by force an ideal Christian commonwealth, with absolute equality and the community of goods. The total defeat of the insurgents at <u>Franken Hausen</u> (May 15, 1525), was followed by the execution of Müntzer and thousands of peasant followers. <u>Martin Luther</u> rejected the demands of the insurgents and upheld the right of Germany's rulers to suppress the uprisings This played a major part in the rejection of his teachings by many German peasants, particularly in the south.

After the Peasants' War (1524/25), a second and more determined attempt to establish a <u>theocracy</u> was made at Münster, in Westphalia (1532–1535). Here a group of prominent citizens, including the Lutheran pastor Bernhard Rothmann, Jan Matthys, and Jan Bockelson ("John of Leiden") had little difficulty in obtaining possession of the town on January 5, 1534. Matthys identified Münster as the "New Jerusalem," and preparations were made, not only to hold what had been gained, but to proceed from Münster toward the conquest of the world.

Claiming to be the successor of David, John of Leiden was installed as king, legalized <u>polygamy</u>, and himself took sixteen wives, one of whom he beheaded himself in the marketplace. <u>Community of goods</u> was also established. After obstinate resistance, the town was taken by the besiegers on June 24, 1535, and then Leiden and some of his more prominent followers were executed in the marketplace.".......,...

It has been common goal of both Islam and Christianity to expunge **Paganism** culture and traditions and do not want to see pagans anywhere in the world, so as to establish world over the rule based on principles of **Prophet Abraham**, but the problem is there are serious differences between each of the monotheistic Abrahamic religions "Judaism, Christians and Islam," while Jews do not have numbers because their population is less than 1% of world's population hence the competition is between Christianity and Islam, the two alleged siblings are estranged therefore fighting hard, less with paganism more between themselves, worst still Islam is fighting more within, the two rival faction of Islam <u>Shiite</u> and <u>Sunni</u> are fighting to finish each other, similar is the problem with Christianity.

After the demise of **Ottoman Empire** in 1918 at the end of 1st world-war, the Islamic caliphate movement was halted, Ottoman Empire was the principle power centre of world's Sunni-Islam. Thereafter to pursue forward the Islamic agenda to establish Islamic caliphate all over the world, a small beginning was made in Egypt, when in 1928 "<u>Hassan al Banna</u>" founded **Muslim Brotherhood** as a transnational Pan-Islamic religious, political and social movement, as time progressed and in years and decades Muslim brotherhood has gained enormous strength, Muslim Brotherhood mottos includes "Believers are but Brothers," "Islam is the Solution", and "Allah is our objective; the Qur'an is the Constitution; the Prophet is our leader; jihad is our way; death for the sake of Allah is our wish." Muslim Brotherhood may have been banned or declared outlawed in several countries including the country of its origin <u>Egypt</u> itself, but, Muslim Brotherhood is an formidable organization and its hierarchy and members dedicatedly works for selfish Islamic causes and its network is spread across the world and has tremendous influence world-wide over Sunni Islamists because of its unmatched mobilizing capabilities, most or almost all of the Islamic jihadists and terror groups around the world have close links and working relations with the Muslim Brotherhood.

The terror attacks on U.S.A. soil on September-11-2001 (9/11) was a strong message to the world that Islam is back in business, and challenged the entire non-Sunni Muslim population of the world, jihadi army commanders saying "*this time it will be fight unto finish,*" only the believers of Sunni Islam will survive remaining folks meaning all non-believers and opponents of Islam will have to perish, in every Islamist jihadists propaganda video and on social media > Muslim clerics communicates to the world "this world is only meant for the true believers (this mean, those who believe in Islam god '**Allah**' and those who pledge allegiance to prophet Muhammad) and remaining population of the world who do not believe in Islamic god Allah are termed as unbelievers" and all unbelievers are infidels and infidels are according to Islam doctrine equal to evil therefore harming the infidels is not considered a sin by Sunni-Muslim instead it is holy duty of each Sunni-Muslim to punish the infidels in extreme situation even killing is permitted.

Islam considers all non-Islamic religious communities and even atheists as infidels, but within Islam the Sunni sect of Islam considers the entire Shiite sect of Islam as heretics, basically the followers Sunni Islam detest every other religions and non-believers, so here let me also emphatically inform that all the notorious Islamic terrorists and jihadists groups "Al Qaeda, Al Shabaab, Boko-Haram, ISIS and Taliban, etc" are **Sunni Muslims**, yes, terrorism is adopted culture of Sunni Islam.

The post Arab spring revolution, most of the Muslim dominated and Muslim ruled countries in west-Asia and north-Africa plunged into serious political and social crisis, the Islamic religious wars that started in 2011 showing no sign whatsoever of abetting, "Syria, Iraq, Yemen and Libya" are the most brutally affected nations, but several other countries in Islamic world, such as "Egypt, Turkey, Tunisia, Lebanon, Pakistan and Afghanistan" as well have experienced extremely high terrorists activities, two denomination of Islam the Shias and Sunnis are fighting war in open battlefield in Iraq, Syria, Lebanon and Yemen, another dominant ethnic community in west-Asia and Arabian region the **Kurdish** as well are not spared, the Kurdish army and guerillas are fighting multiple wars in Iraq, Syria and Turkey against formidable Sunni jihadists groups and official army especially in Turkey.

Political analysts, intellectuals and defence experts views and opinions are sharply divided with regards to so many conflicts, religious wars and terrorism in MENA (middle-east and north-Africa) region of the world. What are those uncanny reason/reasons for such deadly and bloodiest battles and wars to continue for such longer period? Who is responsible for creating problems in Islam and Islamic world? Who benefits most when the Islamic sects fight among themselves? These are some of devastatingly pressing questions and it concerns us all, than another question comes to mind or rather is compelling us to think, "Is Islam imploding or is Islam expanding? Simple questions yet difficult to find answers, political and defence analyst views and opinions are divided, with grave confusion in their mind as they try to ascertain the real reasons and purposes behind brutal religious wars and sectarian violence in Islamic world.

There are two principle theories and potential reason behind 21st century religious wars in Islamic world.

First theory is: "as always the Muslims famous cliché, it is Zionist Christians and Jewish conspiracy to destabilize Islam, vested interest of world's powerful countries, "U.S.A., Russia, Britain, France and other western countries" have orchestrated religious wars to divide and to harm Islam, for commercial purpose these western countries wants to save jobs for the arms and defence equipment manufacturing industries, so sectarian conflicts and religious wars besides terrorism in Islamic world provides opportunity to these powerful and influential countries to sell arms and defence equipment to Islamic countries and make profit, the Zionists wants to save Israel and Israelis, and wants to defame and stigmatize Islam." These are some of the key reasons that leftist leaning and pro-Islamists analysts and political thinkers vehemently cites and argues.

The second theory is: "the Islamic religious wars, sectarian conflicts and terrorism is part of Muslim Brotherhood's and jihadi army commanders vicious long term strategic plan to establish Islamic caliphate all over the world, the rule of believers of Sunni Islam, since 2011 all sectarian conflicts and increased terrorists activities and killings are Sham, Phoney wars are deliberately planned by Islamists, it will significantly and decisively help Sunni-Islam cause in long term, and ultimately help them conquer Europe and America, because savage killings and profound violence in Muslim dominated countries, will provide valid reason for Muslims on pretext of personal safety and security citing deteriorating law and order situation, poverty and persecution as genuine and valid reason for large population of Muslims to migrate to Europe and America, particularly large migration of Muslims to Europe will immensely increase Muslim population in Europe, already Islam as of 2015 is 2nd or 3rd largest religion in Europe, further inflows of migrants will remarkably help populate Europe with Muslims.

Increase Muslim population in Europe and America will create many different kind of social and economic problems, just to put things in perspective, the bigger the social and economic problems, and increase in islamophobia, the more it helps Sunni Islam causes, Muslims are so to say '**smooth-operators**,' they are clever and notorious trouble creators, once Islamists settles and establish their bases and consolidate their position in Europe and America, than in anguish and disgust many Europeans especially the white-skin colour Europeans will be compel to leave Europe and start migrating to other countries in search for better living conditions and exciting economic opportunities, the potential exodus of Europeans from Europe besides slow growth in birth-rate, European women differing pregnancy, and aging European population, and in contrast the increase birth-rate of Muslims, Muslim women getting married at much younger age and becoming mother of 3 or 4 children by the time her age is 28 years, so all these combination of factors will by the end of 21st century and start of 22nd century will make Islam largest religion in Europe and perhaps similar strategy will help Islam considerably increase Muslim population in America, this will help Sunni-Islam conveniently and comprehensively conquer Europe and America."

When Muslim Brotherhood was founded in 1920s, it is alleged that it had planned and prepared a 150 to 200 years long term strategic plan, it has always been goal of Islamists to increase their religion's population, therefore Muslim Brotherhood's allege strategy is to infiltrate as many Muslims inside Europe and America, infiltrate so that Muslims becomes integral part of Europe's and Americas social and economic system, Muslims infiltrates education system and governmental departments, Muslims also participates in political movements and become law makers in different European countries and in U.S., and Canada, Muslims starts working as social workers and starts their own NGO,s to help common people so that to gain sympathy and good-will among local citizens, Muslims gets jobs in banks and financial institutions and of course in mainstream media, so with Muslims well positioned inside Europe and America, they can prepare for final assault to conquer Europe and America,

Western countries in a way inadvertently but determinedly are helping Muslim Brotherhood's nefarious causes, each year, annually western countries such as U.S.A., Britain, European-union, also Japan and China besides international financial institutions like World-Bank and IMF (international monetary fund), all these financial institutions and rich countries provides Tens of billions of U.S.

Dollars in humanitarian and other form of economic help and soft loans to so many Islamic countries, "Turkey, Pakistan, Egypt, Afghanistan and Jordan" are some of the prominent countries that receives Billions of Dollars of economic aid and unprecedented amount of money for other types of humanitarian and development purpose, from such large amount of money that these Islamic countries receives, so, instead of using money productively for helping its citizens and developing their country by improving public infrastructure and starting new industries and businesses to create jobs and business opportunities, significantly large percentage of money is allegedly diverted towards **Islam's jihadi project**, yes, the Billions of Dollars these Muslim countries receives, significantly large amount of money is allegedly diverted and used for financing terrorism and extremism, to wage **religious wars** against non-Muslim communities.

Many Sunni Muslim countries like "Turkey, Pakistan, Saudi Arabia, Egypt, etc" have strategic Defence pact and agreement signed with leading western countries, as part of defence deal powerful industrialized nations such as "U.S.A., Britain and France" provides extensive military aid and supply of sophisticated arms and defence equipment to so many Islamic countries, besides sharing of military secrets and information, more importantly high ranking military officials and security experts renders superlative combative training to official army of several Islamic countries with whom they have defence ties, so, several prominent Sunni Muslim countries are large recipients of America's military aid. Now, this is where trouble begins, the high quality combative training and arms that Sunni Muslim countries receives are than allegedly passed on to the Jihadists or to say Islamic terrorists groups, so, basically it is alleged that all the financial support and economic aid and military training and arms these Islamic countries receives from western countries, allegedly is used against western countries by Sunni Islamic terrorists to destroy western culture and civilization.

The Europeans and Americans so to say *have dig their own grave*, Muslim-brotherhood and other Islamist institutions have successfully outwitted and outsmarted the naïve and gullible American and European politicians, therefore not surprising that even the European and American population have started accusing and cursing their politicians openly blaming them for surrendering before Islam, and politicians as well have started to admit that Europe and America's political and economic system is biased "therefore its feeble and devastatingly vulnerable," Islam is growing in strength, as a consequence of **war on terror** started in 2001 against the so-called radical Islam, on the contrary **"Islam has become more stronger"** than ever before, Europe and America marred by corruption have become increasingly weaker.

As part of their strategy Muslim Brotherhood and Islamic institutions wants it to become **"Islam versus the rest,"** **islamophobia** actually helps Islamic causes, the more a large section of society curses and discriminates Muslims, another section of society vehemently comes forwards to empathize and sympathize with Islam and shows solidarity and pledge their support to Muslims, that's what, makes Sunni-Muslim youngsters more determined to fight holy religious wars.

The terror attacks on American soil in Sept-2001 (9/11) were no ordinary terror attacks but it was a subtle start of the **'third world war,'** Islam versus the rest, the Jihadists have spared no one, every prominent country around the world have been targeted, "London, Mumbai, Madrid, Paris, Nairobi, Brussels, Orlando and San Bernardino" are some of the key cities among so many more cities in so many different parts of the world that have been between 2002 and 2016 experienced savage terror attacks, Sunni terrorists committing barbaric crimes of killing thousands of innocent people, and Islamic jihadi army commanders making it clear that their ambitions and ultimate goal is to **hoist Islamic flag** in centre of **Paris** and in U.S. capital city **Washington**.

*"You are not human if you are not Muslim, if you don't pledge allegiance to 'Allah's apostle **Muhammad**,' than you are infidel and infidels are equal to evil,"* this is how Muslims treat people of non-Muslim communities, though in public Muslims do not admit and agree and if asked they'll vehemently deny, but it is true, that, since childhood every Muslim children are thought to dislike and distrust the infidels (all' non-Muslims), children's are thought and informed "always be on alert and be mentally and physically prepared to serve your religion and make yourself available for Jihad (Islamic holy war or to say religious wars against every non-Islamic communities)."

Muslim Brotherhood project '*Civilization-Jihadist Process*,' means the jihadi army must understand that their work in America and in Europe is kind of grand jihad in eliminating and destroying western civilization from within and sabotaging its miserable house by their hands and the hands of believers of Islam, **"Allah's religion Islam will be victorious and all other religions will be defeated**."

Article title **"The myth of "three Abrahamic faiths,"** "Muslims, just like the unsaved Jews, believe in a "salvation-by-works" religious system. Among the works they believe ushers them into paradise are the fulfillment of their five pillars and the establishment of sharia, a system of geopolitical laws tied to their religion. Within sharia are laws that mandate the subduing of all non-Muslims and women to second-class citizenship or to slavery or to death if they don't comply. Sharia also teaches it is okay for Muslim men to sexually assault anyone who doesn't comply with Islam, regardless of their gender.

So we see in Islam a whole plethora of things that Abraham would never do. Furthermore, the Quran makes many factual errors about Abraham such as the claim that Abraham worshiped at Mecca [Sura 14:37], but he actually worshiped in Hebron [Genesis 13:18]. Abraham did not believe in salvation by works. Abraham rejoiced to see the day of the Lord Jesus Christ, and he saw it and was glad [John 8:56], but Muslims deny Jesus Christ is the Lord and deny that God has a son. Abraham, as Jesus said, was not into killing people who spoke the truth. Muslims who establish sharia believe in killing those who speak the truth of the gospel." Since Muslims do not display the same faith as Abraham, Islam is not an Abrahamic faith."...............

In 2010 Muslims made up 11.7% of the population in Russia, according to rough estimate as of 2014 it has risen to 14%, various statistics proves that when Muslim population hits 5% in any country, that country begins to experience major social problems and violence. "Muslim militants kill the men but take the women to have sex with them. And then after they have used them for a number of months, they're so distraught mentally and physically that then they may let them go or they may kill them (beleaguered women)."

In 15th century came the formation of Muslim Crimean Khanate which occupied the Black Sea shores and the southern steppes of Ukraine. Until the late 18th century, Ottoman forces under "**Gedik Ahmed Pasha**" conquered all of the Crimean peninsula and joined it to the khanate in 1475. During the 16th and 17th centuries, it was an important centre of the slave trade, the Crimean Khanate maintained an enormous slave trade with the Ottoman Empire and the Middle-east between 1500 and 1700A.D in which Muslim merchants exported over 2 million slaves from Russia and Ukraine. Native Russians and Ukrainians, because of their fair skin were in huge demand as slaves (mainly women). Hence targeted for kidnapping and slavery. The Crimean Khanate was a Turkic vassal state of Ottoman Empire during 1478 to 1774, later it was dissolved by Russian empire in 1783. *The Crimean Khanate was one of the many remnants of the Golden Horde, the north-western division of the separated Mongol Empire. Located north of the Black Sea, the Crimean Khanate also proved to be the most lasting remnant. The term "Tatar" derives from an old Mongolian tribe. It eventually came to be a term used by Europeans for the inhabitants and warriors of Mongol Empire as a whole, especially the Golden Horde division.* The majority of Ukrainian Muslims are from Crimean Tatar background. Because of violent nature of Islam and the kidnappings and forced slavery mostly of women, Islam was repressed in Russia starting from Russian conquest of Kazan in 1552 until the rise of Catherine the great in 1762.

As a consumer you should have multiple choices to choose from, <u>consumer is a king</u>, for example: what **milk** you need to drink? Cow milk, Sheep milk, Soy milk or you don't want to drink milk at all instead you prefer drinking fruit juice, it should be your personal choice as to what beverage you want to drink, similarly, what **meat** you would like to eat? Lamb, Beef, Fish or sea-food, again it will be your choice, you eat what you like what taste good to you, no one can or should force you to eat what you don't want to eat and no one can or should stop you from eating what you want to eat. No bank's or financial institution sales agent should try to lure you into <u>borrowing money</u> if there is no genuine requirement, if banker encourages you to borrow money, and if you take **loan** from bank, than, you'll have to spend sleepless nights because you've to repay loan amount back to the bank, or else banking officers will keep sending you notices to recover their loan money, so this is why, let the consumer make choice and let them decide as to what they want to buy and what they're not interested in buying or using.

Like the insurance agents keeps bothering you to buy insurance plan, travel agents entice you to buy travel plan, and sales agents of so many different companies lure you to buy and use their products, similarly various Religion and cults as well compels you and systematically forces you to believe and trust their religion, believe and trust in cult. You're threatened and warned if you are part of the religion that if you disobey and work against the wishes of your religious chieftain, there will be consequences, god will get angry and you'll be destroyed, so various religions as well resort to different kind of cheap flimsy gimmick, to exert pressure on common-people, adopts different strategies to bind the people together and to ensure that people do not gain good enough knowledge, they also work hard to ensure you do not discover the truth or else their shop will shut, so it is all about marketing, how well a religion is branded as a product and promoted, all religions and self-styled **godman** and **goddess-woman** have same strategy when it comes to promoting themselves and to fool the naïve and gullible people, you'll find many fake wicked self-style godman and goddess-woman in India and many other Asian countries perhaps even in Africa, some practice witch-craft.

People who are inexperienced and immature such people are incorrigible hence they trust and believe such master-manipulators and allows them to influence their minds, Religions are nothing but Ponzi schemes. The agents of religious institutions are master-manipulators, they sell false dream and hopes to such vulnerable individuals and preaches them as to "how divine intervention will solve all their problems and prevent them from any possible danger," by fooling the fools they "**rule the roost.**" If you are intelligent and intellectual and have good understanding of life and humanity then you won't allow external sources to influence your mind, modern science, secular scholars and historians do not believe in divine miracles and all unscientific events that have been described in various religions holy-books.

Astronomers do not trust astrologers, **Astrology** is Science and NOT Magic, one of Satan's evil way of deceiving people is with astrology, Zodiacs cannot give you true wisdom nor can fortune teller guide you, be wise and sensible do not allow people to play with your emotions, do not disclose your personal information to these crooks and cheaters like the fortune tellers and astrologers, be smart, you don't allow people to exploit you.

Trust yourself only if you are convince with yourself, if you are convince with yourself and if you firmly believe that you have a good instinct and matured mind and that you are not prone to making any mistakes, only then take the risk of trusting your own-self, "**it is the choices we make and decisions we take**," because the fact is that, our mind (Brain) is our best friend and our worse foe, yes, it's true, our fierce enemy at times can't or won't harm us as much as we harm our own self, it so happens that we humans have tendency to never take blame of our wrong doings on our own-self, instead we make excuses and always try to put blame on someone else for our wrong doings and our misery.

The two most powerful and resourceful religion of our time **Islam** and **Christianity** there rise to power is all because of marketing and excellent PR (Public relation), the council members of both these religious institutions have very well promoted each of these two competing religions, full marks to the managers who've meticulously and skilfully worked in promoting and making Islam and Christianity a phenomenal success.

Touching base with extreme realities of the so-called Abrahamic religions, when we talk of Islam, we always talk of its founder Muhammad, the so-called alleged last prophet of God "Muhammad" is discussed extensively, but, no one really discusses, as in, how Islam was formed? What made Muhammad so great and achieve unprecedented success? All talks of god sending his angel "**Gabriel**" down on earth to communique his message to Muhammad, and so many such imaginative and false stories, unscientific explanation and narratives that we listen and read, but these are all wild imagination and rubbish talks, no secular scholars and intellectuals will ever believe such nonsense theories and stories.

Here is a real true perspective in brief to understand *"how Islam came into being, and, what and who made Muhammad so popular and powerful person ever born on this planet,"* > Muhammad was born into low-income family in either Mecca or Medina modern day part of Saudi Arabia, he belonged to Banu Hashim clan which was part of Quraysh tribe a very powerful tribe in Medina, Muhammad remained unmarried single till he was 25years of age, he use to survive well doing odd job and business deals, even though Muhammad was an absolute illiterate, but it has been written about him that he had excellent oratory and negotiating skills, as it is said that "behind every successful man there is a woman," according to historians have recorded that in 595CE, he married **Khadīja bint Khuwaylid** and she apparently was 15 years older in age than him.

Khadija was also from same Quraysh tribe and was a successful businesswoman, she was a merchant and use to trade large consignment of goods and products, because of her business success she was very influential and respected throughout Arabian region, Khadija was rich, she had staggering personality was shrewd, intelligent, smart, compassionate, use to help and support many people, she was kind and generous woman, but, she did not believe and did not like worshipping idols, but she in her house use to have idol of **Al-Uzza**, "(**Al-'Uzzá** was one of the three chief goddesses of Arabian religion in pre-Islamic times and was worshiped by the pre-Islamic Arabs along with **Allāt** and **Manāt**)," so it was Muhammad's first wife Khadija significantly guided and helped Muhammad gain success, Islam is basically brainchild NOT OF Muhammad's but his first wife Khadija, Khadija was the first person to embrace Islam and she is the one who promoted him as prophet of the believers.

It so happened that during 6th and 7th century people of Arabia and Mesopotamia were fed-up of frequent wars and violence between various kingdoms and warlords, chaotic situation in the Arabian region, "poverty, persecution, high inflation and unemployment," had made people in the region restless as they were feeling insecure, the people wanted peace and a leader to lead them, and Muhammad's first wife being a successful businesswoman having trading business spread across Arabian and Mesopotamia region, hence she was well connected had good contacts in the region, her sources use to constantly update her with information regarding economic and political situation, she was widely travelled and intelligent woman, knew all about peoples aspiration and what is the mood of the people in Arabia and Mesopotamia region, when Khadija realized that people are disenchanted with the political leaders and kings who rule them, she seized an opportunity to exploit the than existing ground situation, and the generous woman that she (Khadija) was, instead of promoting herself and becoming leader and chieftain herself, she used all her resources and the goodwill she had among large majority of people for all her philanthropic work and help she had rendered to so many people, she used it all to her advantage and promoted her husband, she promoted Muhammad as prophet of the believers, and sometime in 610CE launched a peoples movement and named it **Islam** headed by her doting husband Muhammad, Islam was initially a peaceful movement project, majority of people of Hejaz (present day -- Saudi Arabia) liked new peace initiative and gracefully accepted Muhammad as their new leader, many unconditionally pledged allegiance to Muhammad, so Islam was initially started as peaceful movement and had given people a new hope. Muhammad till the time his first wife Khadīja bint Khuwaylid was alive remained loyal to her and did not had any other wife/wives or any extramarital affairs.

"(It is not clear, as to, how many biological children Muhammad had of his own? But, Muhammad for sure had one child from his first wife Khadija bint Khuwaylid had a beautiful daughter her name '**Fatima-Zahra**,' like mother like daughter, Fatima was beautiful, kind-hearted, brave and courageous woman, she married Muhammad's cousin **Ali ibn Abi Talib**, when after death of Muhammad there was rebellion in Islam over his succession and leadership issue, Fatima along with her husband Imam Ali founded **Shiite Islam**, yes, Fatima is founder of Shia Islam, she is mother of the followers of Shia Islam, she had two sons **Imam Hassan** and

Imam Hussein; Fatima resolutely and vehemently opposed <u>the Sunni caliph</u> and Sunni-Islam terrorism).”

But sadly in 620CE Muhammad's first wife Khadija died, and after death of his first wife things dramatically began to change in Islam and unfortunately changed for the worse, till his first wife Khadija was alive Muhammad was disciplined and civilized person, was a very humble man, but soon after death of his first wife, Muhammad was corrupted, Muhammad started receiving advises from all the wrong people, Muhammad broke all his earlier promises and commitments he had made to people of Medina and Hejaz. Islam from peaceful movement became violent and corrupt, Islam became political movement and started attacking and looting villages and resorted to forceful conversions, in wars Islamic army started looting wealth and raping young women and girls, Muhammad himself became self-spoiled he started marrying one woman after another, some record suggest after death of his first wife Khadija, Muhammad married as many as 8 more women, most notable was his marriage to 6 year old kid the voracious **Aisha**, it has been said that he married Aisha when her age was 6 and consummated her when she was just 9 years old, apart from many wives Muhammad also had many concubines, Muhammad voraciously indulged in sex with many women, so initially as it was that Islam was a peaceful religion and its founder Muhammad was a humble man, but after the death of Muhammad's first wife Khadija neither Islam remained peaceful nor did Muhammad remained humble, it will be safe for us to assume “evil took control of both Islam and its founder **Muhammad.**”

One incident I would like mentioning to prove the so-called messenger of peace prophet Mohammed's (Allah's apostles) abhorrent attributes: in one of the many wars which Mohammed fought in 7th century to establish Islam “At the Massacre of Khaybar, Muhammad brutally tortured a Jewish chieftain for extracting information about where he had hidden his treasures. When the treasure was uncovered, the chieftain was beheaded. This chieftain was the husband of the most beautiful Jewish woman of Khaybar, the 17-year-old Safiyaah. Safiyaah's family members had been annihilated by Muhammad at the Banu Qurayza massacre. Now having beheaded her husband, the Prophet took Safiyah as his sex-slave and copulated on the same night." Another incident: "In the massacre of the Jewish Settlement of Bani Mustaliq, Muhammad captured their women and took twenty-year-old Jewish girl, Juwayriya as his sex-slave."

Paganism is and was the ancestor religion of entire humanity, Paganism, or to say, pagan religions were and still are all about meditation and innovation, all pagan religious communities allows their followers to practice rituals the way they like, paganism is not simply about worshipping idols and believing in multiple gods and goddesses, followers of various pagan religions will be seen worshipping everything that mother-nature has/have created, they worship "moon, sun, rivers, earth and cattle etc," for pagans music and dance is sense of individuals that contributes to personal transformation and collective experience of sacred.

Prophet Abraham though himself did promoted one god theory and he was against idol worshiping, but he and his sons were not particularly hostile towards pagans, they did not believe in violence per se, but many hundreds of years later after the death of Abraham and his sons **Isaac** and **Ishmael**, Christian priest owing allegiance to Abraham's son "Isaac" became hostile towards paganism and started preaching idol worshippers are satanic tradition, the fall of paganism is not only to be attributed towards Abrahamic religion Christianity and Islam, but there were many disputes and disagreement among many pagan religions in Europe and in Asia and Africa,

There were too many religions in Rome, in 325 A.D a council was called in an endeavour to amalgamate the many religions of Roman Empire into one.

Christianity plagiarized older myths and legends historicized to suit the Roman catholic church, while combining the numerous religions existing at the time (Krishna, Horus, Mithraism, Osirian, Isis and many other mystery religions), for unity and to stop all conflict between the numerous religions.

Eusebius (Bishop of Caesarea in Palestine "father of church") Eusebius who was **Constantine** friend, hence, he helped <u>Roman Emperor Constantine</u> establish Christianity."

In fact Christianity came into effect because of problems in paganism, when first Christianity and later Islam began to flourish, that's when, brutal fall of paganism began, many pagan religions and people instead of surrendering before Christianity and Islam, they started to migrate eastwards, many pagan followers migrated to India, so as to avoid persecution and for them to continue with their traditions, paganism did survived in some African countries and also in remote parts of Europe, but paganism has survived in India, most of tradition from ancient Egypt and Rome, most of the gods and goddesses and rituals that were earlier practice in Egypt and Roman Europe in ancient era, are still being practiced in India and several East-Asian countries like for example Cambodia, Burma (Myanmar) and Thailand.

When Christianity and Islam became powerful religion and started expanding, many primitive era records and ancient civilization history was destroyed, world over schools and universities largely funded and controlled by churches and Christian missionaries or by Islamic institutions hence text books were or have been written providing incorrect information, for their own selfish purpose the Christian priests and Muslim clerics are allegedly responsible for destroying ancient history and archaeological structures and many other facts about ancient paganism and their culture and traditions, not just primitive era records of we modern humans and paganism, but it seems there was allege similarity and connection between modern humans and **Neanderthal**, it is therefore alleged even Neanderthal followed and practice few similar rituals like pagans. Christians and Muslims for their own survival resorted to massive disinformation campaign, and religious institutions have misinformed masses about primitive era history and everything that nature had created.

Article title **"why talk about the Neanderthal?"** describes; "Much archaeological material has been destroyed, intentionally or by accident, or is being kept secret, or has been 'lost', or is deemed not important enough by the scholars to discuss. They 'forget' to mention so much to us, to the public.

It is no coincident that the first 'archaeologists' were all priests, who often systematically went forth to destroy all evidence suggesting that Europeans had had any type of culture prior to Christianity. Some were probably even doing this not at all because they had an interest in what we today call archaeology, but solely to destroy all evidence undermining their own version of the world's history. "Quickly, dig up the grave and destroy everything you find, before somebody else finds it!"

When priests found Neanderthal skulls, they did the same. They found large skulls that obviously had held brains *larger* than those of modern humans, so they had to do something! Both those believing in the theory of evolution and the Judeo-Christians claiming that Pagan Europe was primitive had a serious problem. So they *intentionally* misplaced the spinal column and the lower jaw, making the Neanderthal look ape-like. *This image has been proven to be false already*, but the image of the Neanderthal as some ape-like creature with a protruding face remains, and when you visit Neanderthal sites most (but thankfully not all) of the guides still talk about them as if they were like that. When you point at the fact that this is wrong, most of them already know, but for some reason keep telling the 'well established' lie instead. I don't know why they still do, even when they know they are wrong, but they do. Yes, in reality **the Neanderthal didn't have a protruding face at all**, and the supra-orbital ridge found (in adults only) can *still* occasionally be found in modern adult Europeans."................

The faith of most religious Jews is called **Judaism**, and it is the oldest of three monotheistic religions (this means, religions serving only one God), Judaism is parent of "Christianity and Islam," Prophet Abraham is considered father of all three religion "Judaism, Christianity and Islam," Abrahamic religions proclaim that there is only one God, whose name is **Yahweh**, "(now they' Abrahamic religions on what basis only they know, but have no explanation because they know nothing, yet they have determined that **God's** gender is <u>male</u>, so they address god as' he and him)" He (Yahweh) is the creator and ruler of the universe, he revealed his law **"the Torah"** to the Jewish people (who were at that time known as Hebrew people) and he (the alleged god' Yahweh) chose them (Hebrew people) to be light for all humanity, the Torah contains 613 commands which have been summed up to **Ten Commandments**.

Prophet Abraham's religious family members have no love only hatred and distrust for each other, Jewish people can be considered as elder brothers and sisters of Christians and Muslims, little love perhaps Christians have for Jewish people, but Muslims profoundly dislike and hate both their supposed siblings, more intense is their hatred targeted towards Jewish community, so there is minimum agreement and maximum disagreement and distrust among each of the three monotheistic religions (Judaism, Christianity and Islam,); anti-Semitism especially European Christians dislike Jews, for economic reason alleges that Jews are extremely wealthy and deprives other communities from obtaining wealth and that Jews believe in controlling the world's economy, also many Christians have ill-feelings for Jews because they believe that Jews killed <u>Jesus Christ</u>, Jews are racially discriminated by the Europeans especially in pre-World-war 2 era, alleging Jews are inferior race, Jews argue that they are not a **race** but Judaism is a religion and person from any race and region can become a Jewish and practice Judaism.

"Between the years 250 CE and 1948 CE - a period of 1,700 years - Jews have experienced more than eighty expulsions from various countries in Europe - an average of nearly one expulsion every twenty-one years. Jews were expelled from England, France, Austria, Germany, Lithuania, Spain, Portugal, Bohemia, Moravia and seventy-one other countries." but the biggest point of discontent and disagreement is that Christians wants the Jewish people to accept '<u>Jesus as son of god</u>' and agree to the fact that Jesus of Nazareth is a **messiah** and savior of Israelis, the Jewish community is adamant not to consider Jesus as a messiah or ready to believe and dismisses claim that Jesus is one of the trinity god' the son of god.

The Christian doctrine of the **Trinity** that God is three consubstantial persons the Father the Son (Jesus Christ), and the Holy Spirit —as "one God in three Divine Persons." Both Islam and Judaism strongly disagrees to Christianity's Trinity concept of God.

Following their kosher meal tradition and as per their Halal (legitimate) diet > Islam and Jewish folks restrain from eating **Pork**, but Christians relish on eating Pork meat, Jewish and Muslim men compulsory practice ritual of **Circumcision**, but majority Christian community term circumcision as discriminatory, very few Christians practice male circumcision, in some Christian ruled countries male circumcision is declared unlawful and illegal.

But there are even bigger dispute and disagreement between these three Abrahamic religion, in Hebrew bible as well in Torah god name is mention as Yahweh, Muslims insist god name is 'Allah,' Islam claims "there is no god but Allah and religion of Allah is the only pure and legitimate religion and every other religions are flawed," Islamic holy-book **Quran** is to the large extent copied or inspired from **Bible** and **Torah**, it is alleged that Islamists authors of Quran have copied Bible and Torah but have heavily edited and amended several critically important verses. Therefore, Islam stubbornly points out errors and deviations introduced to the original message of Jesus and Moses, Islamists strongly argues that Bible contains many contradictions and unscientific explanations.

Muslims categorically says, that, the Quran, in by itself, is the most important miracle that Prophet Mohammad has brought to humanity. Since Prophet Mohammad was intended to be the last prophet and the Quran was the last message, God decided to give people a unique miracle that can be examined and experienced by not only people who lived at the time of the prophet, but for the hundreds of years to come. Muslims claims "Quran is word of god as recited to Prophet Muhammad through the angel Gabriel." So, it was natural for God to choose Quran to be such a miracle.

However religious scholars of Judaism and Christianity strongly objects to tall claims of Islamists, and points out fault in Quran, the Jewish and Christian religious scholars points out several fault in Quran and goes on to say that Islam holy-book Quran is a bluff, so heated debate to prove each other wrong and prove themselves right, Islamists in a way even have snubbed god, and tried to challenge the wisdom of god, otherwise Islamists says "the almighty God is infallible and can never make mistake, god is kind and forgiving," but in its bid to prove that Islam is true and every other religions and their holy-books are flawed and faulty, Muslims agree that both Jews and Christians are part of Abrahamic clan and same god Allah has created all three of these religion, but Islamists argues that God made serious mistakes and error while creating Jews and Christians (such Muslim claims are both annoying and as well childish and laughable), God had initially made errors in Hebrew and Christian bible, which apparently God through his last prophet Muhammad have corrected it all, therefore those who pledge allegiance to Allah's prophet Muhammad and accept Quran as the only true guide and constitution book and follows the principles of Quran, those people are genuine and true believers, and rest of the people who oppose Quran and prophet Muhammad are infidels and infidels are as good as evil.

Islamists arrogantly disregards non-Muslims, says, that, both the Jews and Christians are ugly creature of God, people the followers of both these communities are filthy and dirty not worth calling them humans, Allah made serious mistakes when he created the Jews and Christians and later he corrected his mistakes when he created Islam, therefore, only the followers of Islam are **holiest** and **real humans**, and Allah (Islamic god and also Muslims considers Allah as real God of Abrahamic religions) will open doors of **Paradise** for each Muslims, heaven for Muslims and **fire of hell** for the Christians and Jews.

Muslims have brazen double standards, while Sunni-Muslims mince no words, and without any regret or shame calls every non-Sunni Muslim communities and those people who do not believe in Islamist doctrine as **Kafir** (infidels), an according to Islamic doctrine Kafirs (infidels) are evil worshippers, and according to hardline Islamist belief harming and punishing or even going to an extent of killing the infidels is considered as holy duty of every practicing devout Muslim, Muslim clerics and priests on record preach and advices to followers of Islam that everything that is produced by non-Islamic communities or atheists (unbelievers) is

Haraam (illegitimate), hence Muslims should restrain themselves from using and consuming foods items and many other consumer products and material that are produced by Pagan, Jewish and other non-believers of Islam.

You may listen such slogans in most of the Islamic countries as well in Muslim dominated countries and localities, Muslims shouting <u>death to America</u>, <u>boycott Israel,</u> Muslims are severely critical towards Jewish community, and also we hear from Muslims many other slogans condemning non-Muslims and idol worshippers, but, members of Muslim communities and followers of Islam when they are wounded and injured or suffering from illness to heal their wounds and to cure diseases they consume medicines which apparently are researched and developed by Jewish scientists, and manufactured in Jewish or Pagan (idol and nature worshipers) owned factories. Muslims makes extensive use of scientific technologies which again are researched, design and developed by Jewish or atheists and most likely manufactured in Jewish or Christian owned factories.

Similarly Islamic countries and Muslim institutions graciously accept economic and financial aid and help from non-Islamic countries governments (U.S.A., Japan and European governments provides Billions of Dollars in economic aid and other incentives to so many Islamic and Muslim dominated countries) and financial institutions, so accepting money and donations from financial institutions which are controlled by Jewish or atheists is OK for Muslim folks, seeking asylum and refuge in non-Islamic country is OK, but, yet Muslims are not ready to concede, they continue pouring stream of invective against non-Sunni Muslim communities, Muslims will take money, accept economic aid packages from non-Muslim governments and institutions and use their technology and consume medicines, yet Muslims brazenly calls non-Muslim communities "Kafir" (infidel) and vociferate for total destruction of unbelievers or to say they (Sunni-Muslims) vows to eliminate anyone and everything that is non-Islamic.

Erroneous assumptions and childish behaviour of each of these two prominent religion **Christianity** and **Islam** are only resulting in increased crime rates and frequent bloody religious wars in so many different parts of the world, it is becoming all to frequent to see images of **Sunni Muslim jihadi terrorists** gate crashing and firing bullets to kill non-Sunni Muslim people, ruining peace of mind of entire world's population, Sunni jihadists attacking "nightclubs, targeting gays and lesbians joints, exploding bombs at beach resorts and hotels, attacking airports and city squares."

Sunni-Muslims have problems with everything, they've problems with "Beer, wine, bikini clad girls, women wearing skimpy clothes like short frock, discos, all types of music, artefacts, they dislike Jewish community, they hate atheists and detest gays and lesbians, in super-markets they want Halal food, in cosmetic shops they want Halal (legitimate as per Islamic law or permitted by Sharia) cosmetic items Perfumes and lipsticks without any alcohol contains, in airlines while travelling they (Muslims) insist Halal food is served to them, they want prayer hall or some kind of adjustment be made so as to offer their regular prayers at workplace or you'll see them praying right on street pavement or on the corner of the road or in case while travelling they pray on railway platform or at airport lounge," damn it these Muslims are so demanding and fussy want preferential treatments and privileges, irrespective and regardless of which country they live in, they want everything as per their religious permissible rule, if their religion 'Islam' restricts them from so many things, than for "what purpose do these Muslims migrate to non-believers progressive European and American countries? Why can't Muslims live as per their traditions in their own respective Islamic countries and do what they like best doing? And allow the rest of the world's non-Muslim population live in peace.

The Muslim institutions and religious council hierarchy, clerics and politicians for generations have successfully indoctrinated minds of naïve and gullible individuals; here in an interesting article to have better and scientific perspective of who Allah (the Muslim God) actually is and what is its significance Article title **"Allah – The Moon God" The Archeology of the Middle East**"- "The religion of Islam has as its focus of worship a deity by the name of *"Allah."* The Muslims claim that Allah in pre-Islamic times was the biblical God of the Patriarchs, prophets, and apostles. The issue is thus one of continuity. Was *"Allah"* the biblical God or a pagan god in Arabia during pre-Islamic times? The Muslim's claim of continuity is essential to their attempt to convert Jews and Christians for if *"Allah"* is part of the flow of divine revelation in Scripture, then it is the next step in biblical religion. Thus we should all become Muslims. But, on the other hand, if Allah was a pre-Islamic pagan deity, then its core claim is refuted. Religious claims often fall before the results of hard sciences such as archeology. We can endlessly speculate about the past or go and dig it up and see what the evidence reveals. This is the only way to find out the truth concerning the origins of Allah. As we shall see, the hard evidence demonstrates that the god Allah was a pagan deity. In fact, he was the Moon-god who was married to the sun goddess and the stars were his daughters.

Archaeologists have uncovered temples to the Moon-god throughout the Middle East. From the mountains of Turkey to the banks of the Nile, the most wide-spread religion of the ancient world was the worship of the Moon-god. In the first literate civilization, the Sumerians have left us thousands of clay tablets in which they described their religious beliefs. As demonstrated by Sjoberg and Hall, the ancient Sumerians worshipped a Moon-god who was called many different names. The most popular names were Nanna, Suen and Asimbabbar. His symbol was the crescent moon. Given the amount of artifacts concerning the worship of this Moon-god, it is clear that this was the dominant religion in Sumeria. The cult of the Moon-god was the most popular religion throughout ancient Mesopotamia. The Assyrians, Babylonians, and the Akkadians took the word Suen and transformed it into the word Sin as their favorite name for the Moon-God. As Prof. Potts pointed out, *"Sin is a name essentially Sumerian in origin which had been borrowed by the Semites."*

In ancient Syria and Canna, the Moon-god Sin was usually represented by the moon in its crescent phase. At times the full moon was placed inside the crescent moon to emphasize all the phases of the moon. The sun-goddess was the wife of Sin and the stars were their daughters. For example, Istar was a daughter of Sin. Sacrifices to the Moon-god are described in the Pas Shamra texts. In the Ugaritic texts, the Moon-god was sometimes called Kusuh. In Persia, as well as in Egypt, the Moon-god is depicted on wall murals and on the heads of statues. He was the Judge of men and gods. The Old Testament constantly rebuked the worship of the Moon-god (Deuteronomy 4:19; 17:3; II Kings 21:3, 5; 23:5; Jeremiah 8:2; 19:13; Zephaniah 1:5, etc.) When Israel fell into idolatry, it was usually the cult of the Moon-god. As a matter of fact, everywhere in the ancient world, the symbol of the crescent moon can be found on seal impressions, steles, pottery, amulets, clay tablets, cylinders, weights, earrings, necklaces, wall murals, etc. In Tell-el-Obeid, a copper calf was found with a crescent moon on its forehead. An idol with the body of a bull and the head of man has a crescent moon inlaid on its forehead with shells. In Ur, the Stele of Ur-Nammu has the crescent symbol placed at the top of the register of gods because the Moon-god was the head of the gods. Even bread was baked in the form of a crescent as an act of devotion to the Moon-god. The Ur of the Chaldees was so devoted to the Moon-god that it was sometimes called Nannar in tablets from that time period.

A temple of the Moon-god has been excavated in Ur by Sir Leonard Woolley. He dug up many examples of moon worship in Ur and these are displayed in the British Museum to this day. Harran was likewise noted for its devotion to the Moon-god. In the 1950's a major temple to the Moon-god was excavated at Hazer in Palestine. Two idols of the Moon god were found. Each was a stature of a man sitting upon a throne with a crescent moon carved on his chest. The accompanying inscriptions make it clear that these were idols of the Moon-god. Several smaller statues were also found which were identified by their inscriptions as the "daughters" of the Moon-god. What about Arabia? As pointed out by Prof. Coon, *"Muslims are notoriously loath to preserve traditions of earlier paganism and like to garble what pre-Islamic history they permit to survive in anachronistic terms."*...........

A fierce debate is now raging between Christians, Muslims, and secular intellectuals in the world media and on the Internet. And if the American invasion of Iraq has taught us anything, it is that we must expect the political and religious tensions to continue to rise over the coming decades, with increased military spending, an escalation in global conflict, and the possibility of nuclear terrorism. Our interpretation of the history of ideas and beliefs began around three thousand years ago, when the Jewish priesthood took advantage of the newly discovered power of alphabetic writing to craft a detailed mythology about a single God of creation. Using myths about miracles, the priests succeeded in uniting their population under a single belief and giving them a practical set of laws and values. Guided by their communal faith, the Jewish people themselves became the law-keepers, and under the watchful eye of a powerful priesthood, kings were held accountable to the same standards as commoners. Greek storytellers also adopted alphabetic writing, but they were unable to make their traditional myths about a family of selfish gods sound convincing, and interaction between the gods was often unfriendly, and so Greek religious morality was largely ineffective.

I found this article title; "**Is Kaaba in Mecca actually a Lord Shiva Lingam?**" interesting as it provides best perspective about the Islamic links with Paganism, as it is widely believed and perceived that Islam's holiest pilgrimage site "**Kaaba**" in Mecca was actually a Pagan Temple with 360 idols of Pagan Gods, the idols apparently were allegedly destroyed when Islamic army in 7th century conquered the Mecca and Medina (Now, part of Saudi Arabia) and established Islam religion, here have a listen; "Long before Islam came in to existence, Kaaba, in Mecca in Saudi Arabia was a pilgrimage site. The word Kaaba might have come from the Tamil Language which originated around 1700BC. In Tamil Nadu Kabaalishwaran temple is Lord Shiva's temple and Kabaali refers to Lord Shiva. The black stone at Kaaba is held sacred and holy in Islam and is called "Hajre Aswad" from the Sanskrit word Sanghey Ashweta or Non-white stone. The Shiva Lingam is also called Sanghey Ashweta. So what is in Kaaba could be the same what Hindus worship. The pedestal Maqam-E-Ibrahim at the centre of the Kaaba is octagonal in shape. In Hinduism, the pedestal of Brahma the creator is also octagonal in shape. Muslim pilgrims visiting the Kaaba temple go around it seven times. In no other mosque does the circumambulation prevail. Hindus invariably Circumambulate or Pradakshina, around their deities. This is yet another proof that the Kaaba shrine is a pre-Islamic. In Shiva temples Hindus always practice circumambulation or Pradakshina. Just as in Hinduism, the custom of circumambulation by Muslim pilgrims around the entire Kaaba building seven times shows that the claim that in Islam they don't worship stones is not true.

Allah was one of the deities in Kaaba long before Islam was founded. It might come as a stunning revelation to many that the word 'ALLAH' itself is Sanskrit. In Sanskrit language Allah, Akka and Amba are synonyms. They signify a goddess or mother. The term 'ALLAH' forms part of Sanskrit chants invoking goddess Durga, also known as Bhavani, Chandi and Mahishasurmardini. The Islamic word for God is., therefore, not an innovation but the ancient Sanskrit appellation retained and continued by Islam. Allah means mother or goddess and mother goddess.

The King Vikramaditya inscription was found on a gold dish hung inside the Kaaba shrine in Mecca, proving beyond doubt that the Arabian Peninsula formed a part of his Indian Empire. (Ref: page 315 of a volume known as 'Sayar-ul-Okul' treasured in the Makhtab-e-Sultania library in Istanbul, Turkey). King Vikrama's preachers had succeeded in spreading the Vedic Hindu sacred scriptures in Arabia and Arabs were once followers of the Indian Vedic way of life. The annual fair known as OKAJ which used to be held every year around the Kaaba temple in Mecca and the present annual hajj of the Muslims to the Kaaba is of earlier pre-Islamic congregation. Even to this day ancient Siva emblems can be seen. It is the Shankara (Siva) stone that Muslim pilgrims reverently touch and kiss in the Kaaba. Muslims shave their head and beard and don special sacred attire that consists of two seamless sheets of white cloth. One is to be worn round the waist and the other over the shoulders. Both these rites are remnants of the old Vedic practice of entering Hindu temples clean and with holy seamless white sheets. According to the Encyclopedia Britannica, the Kaaba has 360 idols. Traditional accounts mention that one of the deities among the 360 destroyed when the place was stormed was that of Saturn; another was of the Moon and yet another was one called Allah. That shows that in the Kaaba the Arabs worshipped the nine planets in pre-Islamic days. In India the practice of 'Navagraha' puja, that is worship of the nine planets, is still in vogue. Two of these nine are Saturn and Moon. In India the crescent moon is always painted across the forehead of the Siva symbol. Since that symbol was associated with the Siva emblem in Kaaba it came to be grafted on the flag of Islam.

The Hindu Vedic letter in Sanskrit "OM" if seen in a mirror one can see the Arabic numbers 786 and this is the most sacred number for Muslims and copies of the Arabic Koran have the mysterious figure 786 imprinted on them. In their ignorance simply they do not realize that this special number is nothing more than the holiest of Vedic symbols misread and none of the Arabic scholar has been able to determine how they chose 786 as the sacred for them. In short Muslims are also going around Siva Lingam at Kaaba, seven times as Hindus go around it seven times.

A few miles away from Mecca are a big signboard which bars the entry of any non-Muslim into the area. This is a reminder of the days when the Kaaba was stormed and captured solely for the newly established faith of Islam. The object in barring entry of non-Muslims was obviously to prevent its recapture. Kaaba is clothed in a black shroud. This custom also originated from the days when it was thought necessary to discourage its recapture by camouflaging it.

Another Hindu tradition associated with the Kaaba is that of the sacred stream Ganga (sacred waters of the Ganges river). According to the Hindu tradition Ganga is also inseparable from the Shiva emblem as the crescent moon. Wherever there is a Siva emblem, Ganga must co-exist. True to that association a sacred fount exists near the Kaaba. Its water is held sacred because it has been traditionally regarded as Ganga since pre-Islamic times (Zam-Zam water)."…..

It is a well-known fact that Islam adapted the Pagan practice of fasting. There is a Hadith in Sahih Bukhari that mentions the ritual. '*Ashura* was a day on which the tribe of Quraish used to fast in the pre-Islamic period of ignorance. The Prophet also used to fast on this day. So when he migrated to Medina, he fasted on it and ordered (the Muslims) to fast on it. When the fasting of Ramadan was enjoined, it became optional for the people to fast or not to fast on the day of *Ashura*.' The fasting for *Ashura* (10th of Muharram) originated from a Quraish Pagan practice. Ramadan fasting came later from *Sabian* tradition. *Sabians* are mentioned in several verses of the Quran along with Christians and Jewish. *Sabians*, a non-Muslim Iraqi tribe, believed in monotheism, observed fasting 30 days a year, and prayed 5 times a day.

The Sabians, who were pagans in the Middle-East, were identified in two groups, the Mandaeans and the Harranians. The Mandaeans lived in Iraq during the 2nd century A.D. as they continue to do today, they worshipped multiple gods, or "light personalities." The other group, considered as Sabians were the Harranians. They worshipped Sin, the moon, as their main deity, but they also worshipped planets and other deities.

In article "**under Enlightenment, Islam**" has written; "there's more. It turns out that the pagans also prayed five times a day facing towards the Kaaba. And before they prayed, they performed ritual washing or ablution. And most curiously, the pagans also had a common saying that was the central tenet of many of their faiths: "There is no god but God." For the unfamiliar, the first pillar of Islam is identical to this mantra with one slight revision: "There is no god but God; and Mohammad is his last messenger." And of course, it's well known that Muslims are required to pray five times daily after performing ritual washing.

So if the ritual of Ramadan was originally conceived to honour the deity of the Moon, why were these practices not destroyed like the idols in the Kaaba? Just like Constantine combined Roman paganism with Christianity to ensure peace & secure power, so too has Islam cannibalized its pagan predecessors to woo converts. Modern Muslims are completely oblivious to the fact that they are actually celebrating the death and rebirth of the Moon deity in accordance with ancient pagan astrology."...........

According to Hadith Bukhari 3:43:658 Narrated by "Abdullah bin Masud:" The Prophet entered Mecca and (at that time) there were three hundred-and-sixty idols around the Kaaba. He started stabbing the idols with a stick he had in his hand and reciting: "Truth (Islam) has come and Falsehood (disbelief) has vanished."

There were 360 idols around the Kaaba. The pilgrimages to the Kaaba were all pagan pilgrimages, the ritual processions around the Kaaba were part of pagan beliefs and custom, the white robes worn by the pilgrims were from pagan faiths, the veneration of the Kaaba and black stone are derived from pagan rituals and beliefs. Pagans called out the names of their pagan gods as they circled the Kaaba, today, Muslims call out Allah's name. Pagans ran between the nearby hills, Muhammad authorized Muslims to do that in the Quran, and probably ran between the hills himself.

Excerpts from article **"Christianity is fake, Here is proof,"** describes like Islam, similarly Christianity is closely linked to paganism; "Pagan's/Wiccan's have been attacked and prosecuted by Christians/Catholics for many years. Yet, Little do they know, that their whole religion is a plagiarized version of the pagan religion itself, Many don't see this.. The holidays, Like **"Christmas, Easter, Halloween, thanksgiving."** They were pagan religion's festivals long before Christianity was in the thoughts of men.. Samhain, Is today's Halloween, The pagan's Yule holiday, is Christianity's Christmas, Which both coincidentally is the same day.. As is Samhain.. Notice the word Yule used.. A very common pagan word, used for Christmas.. It is The Holiday is a celebration for Rebirth and Life.. The Holiday Imbolic, Is today's groundhog day.. Still..

The Pagan Holiday Eostara is Christian's Easter.. The holiday is a celebration of rebirth.. Which is a coincidence considering it is considered the day that Jesus Rose again.. Our Religion Mabon.. Is Christian's thanks' giving.. Which is also a day for giving thanks'..

Now off to another point.. Christian symbols.. Christian Symbols you see today are also Pagan Symbols.. Like the **Cross** that Jesus died on.. The cross is considered to a pagan, as the Cross of the Zodiac, The circle around the centre point of the cross represents the sun.. Which is where the idea, of' Jesus the son of god. The Fish.. The fish that Jesus drew on the ground, Is also the same symbol used to represent Pagan astrology's symbol of the ages.. Which in this case, is the age of Pisces, Which we are still in today.

Now, this is where the real proof comes in. The story of Jesus, Believe it or not, The story of Jesus has been told Thousands of years before Christian's Jesus was born, The list of how many people share the same story and same trait's is seemingly endless.. Which makes me believe, that there was a man somewhere that has done the same thing has him.. One example of many.. Horus was also born of the virgin Isis, He is the Only Begotten son of Osiris, His Foster father was Seb, Also meaning Jo-seph,

Him and Jesus are of Royal Descent, Both born in a cave, An Angel came to both, and Warned Isis of her virgin birth, 3 king's came to Jesus following a star to the east, 3 solar deities, Followed a star to the east, to find Horus, Mother Isis was told at the birth of Horus "Come, thou goddess Isis, hide thyself with thy child.". As Joseph, Father of Jesus was told "Arise and take the young child and his mother and flee into Egypt.". Both were teacher's at the age of 12, They were both Baptized at the age of 30, Horus Baptized by Anup, as Jesus baptized by John the Baptist, Both Anup, and John were Beheaded. Horus and Jesus both performed many miracles, such as Raising the dead, Water to wine, Walking on water, and many more.. Later He was Betrayed by A close friend and Disciple, To then be crucified and then cast into a tomb.. Both resurrected 3 day's later, to then later descend into the heaven's.. Keep in mind, This is only one story that is similar to the story of Jesus.. And also.. Much Much older.. There are so many, it would take entirely too long to go through it all, Although, if you wish to research yourself.. I will list a few name's... Odin of the Norse, Mithra, Krishna, Gautama a.k.a.Buddha, Attis , Zoroaster, Dionysus, Quetzaloatl, Tammuz, Alestis, Esus, Bel, Bali, Orpheus, Iao and Wittoba.. Keep in mind. .There are many many more "…….."

The name "Easter" comes from occult and pagan celebration of their spring goddess "Eostre and Ishtar," The Babylonians and other Pagan cultures had a spring festival in honour of their goddess of spring and rebirth. **Easter Friday** is also a pagan celebration timed to be on the third full "Moon Day" from the start of the year.

In an Article title "**India's God Krishna was king of Jerusalem!**" provides clear perspective for us to understand who Jesus Christ is /was and truth about Christianity; "**What** a strange world in which we live! The Catholic Church has always known that Christianity did not begin with Jesus Christ, but yet it tries to make us think it did.

St. Augustine of Hippo (354-430 AD) wrote: "This, in our day, is the Christian religion, not as having been unknown in former times, but as having recently received that name."

Eusebius of Caesarea (circa 283-371 AD) said: "The religion of Jesus Christ is neither new nor strange."

In *Anacalypsis,* The 17th century British orientalist and iconoclast, Godfrey Higgins, insisted that Christianity was already firmly in place in both the West and the East, many centuries before Jesus Christ was born. He said, The Crestians or Christians of the West probably descended directly from the Buddhists, rather than from the Brahmins. (Vol. 2, pp 438, 439.)

The existence of the Christians both in Europe and India, (existed) long anterior to the Christian era... (Vol 2, p. 202.) I think the most blind and credulous of devotees must allow that we have the existence of the Cristna of the Brahmins in Thrace, many hundred years before the Christian era-the birth of Jesus Christ. (Book X, p. 593.)

"Melito (a Christian bishop of Sardis) in the year 170, claims the patronage of the emperor, for the now so-called Christian religion, which he calls "our philosophy," on account of its high antiquity, has having been imported from countries lying beyond the limits of the Roman empire, in the region of his ancestor Augustus, who found the importation ominous of good fortune to his government." This is an absolute demonstration that Christianity did not originate in Judea, which was a Roman province, but really was an exotic oriental fable, imported from India, and that Paul was doing as he claimed, viz: preaching a God manifest in the flesh who had been "believed in the world" centuries before his time, and a doctrine which had already been preached "unto every creature under heaven." (*Bible Myths and Their Parallels in Other Religions;* T. W. Doane, p. 409.)

Religious historians have for hundreds of years struggled to find out how and why the stories about Jesus and Krishna, who were born 2,000 years apart, are so nearly identical.

- Both Christ and Krishna descended from Noah.
- The future births of both messiahs were predicted ahead of time.
- Christ was descended from Abraham
- Krishna was the father of Abraham (Brahma).
- Christ was at once a Koresh, a Hebrew, and a Yehudi.
- Krishna was at once a Kurus, an Abhira, and a Yadava.
- Christ was an incarnation of Yah-Veh.
- Krishna was at once an incarnation of Vishnu and Shiva.
- Christ's first name, Jesus, was Yeshua.
- A title of Krishna, meaning "love; devotion," was Yesu. Even today, many Hindu parents name their sons, Yesu Krishna.
- Both men were born of virgins and in a stable.
- Krishna's mother was named Devaki.
- Jesus mother was called Mary.
- Krishna did not have an earthly father as such, but a protector, named Vasudeva.

- Jesus did not have an earthly father as such, but a mortal protector named Joseph.
- An evil king tried to kill Christ and Krishna when they were both infants.
- To protect the infant Jesus, Joseph and Mary took him to Maturai, Egypt.
- To protect the infant Krishna, his parents, Vasudeva and Devaki, took him to Mathura, India.
- It was predicted that both men would die to atone for the sins of their people.
- As you have probably noticed, they took refuge in places having almost identical names.
- Both men preached to their people.
- Christ was crucified and then resurrected. Krishna was killed by a hunter's arrow and impaled on a tree. Later, he returned to life.
- Christ was crucified in Jerusalem.
- Some Hindu scholars think that Krishna died in Jerusalem, having gone there when his coastal city of Dwarka sank under the sea. Others say he went to Iraq.
- Christ appeared after his "death." Krishna appeared after his "death."
- Both of them have a major holiday dedicated to them on December 25th.
- Christ had a female admirer named Mary Magdalene. Krishna had a female admirer named Marya Maghadalena.

Fanatically sectarian Christians and Hindus alike militantly reject the idea that the stories of these two deities are related. The Christians accuse the Hindus of blurring their identities on purpose. Some even claim that the Devil himself is the culprit. The Hindus reciprocate accordingly. Unfortunately, neither side can prove or disprove anything. In this article, I will attempt to clear up this mystery once and for all.

The Hindu Equivalent of our Old Testament Story of Abraham.

The story begins with our Abraham or Brahma as the Hindus called him. His father was Lord Krishna; his brother was Mahesh a.k.a Maheshvara who would be our Moses (Heb: *Moshe*).

The Hindu triad consists of the Gods Brahma, the equivalent of our God, and Gods Shiva and Vishnu. Actually Shiva and Vishnu are one and the same deities. Together, they are Brahma (God). Today, in India, there are only two temples dedicated to God Brahma because the Hindus say mankind is not yet ready to worship such a lofty concept.

Hindu Proof That Jesus Is the Son of God!

The Bible tells us that Jesus was both Shiva and Vishnu, for Jesus' biblical names are *Isa/Isha* (Shiva), *Yeshua* (Skt. Yishvara, pronounced in Sanskrit as Yeshwara), Kristos, and Yesu, another name of Krishna. Even in India, Lord Krishna was and still is called *Yesu Krishna and Kristna.* These names prove to us that Jesus was both Shiva and Vishnu, thus making Jesus the begotten son of the Unbegotten-Brahma."……….

There is nothing divine, unique or exclusive in Christianity and Islam, with regards to Islam and Christianity, I have this say "**Old Wine filled in even Older Bottle > than, re-labelled >re-branded > repackaged and then through extensive sales promotion and marketing sold to the consumers and frivolous consumers without going into details or verifying authenticity, started buying and consuming wine.**" People buy medicines and other food items without checking expiry dates and other vital information regarding the product, sexy girls and handsome men models services used for brand promotion to entice people to buy products. Similarly people starts believing in religion and cult or trust fortune tellers and astrologers, fools follow the foolish without applying their own mind and do not bother to establish the truth.

Therefore both the two major religion "Islam and Christianity" are copycat, were formed for political purpose, to gain territories and to obtain wealth and power. Abrahamic religions or for that matter every other religion and cults are chaotic only spreading superstition, especially Christianity and Islam are "**Satanic Fraud.**" Jesus the Nazareth allegedly is imaginative and fictitious character, in all fairness

Christianity is and was created and formed by **Roman Emperor Constantine** for wider political and economic purpose.

Article titled: *"The assortment of Christian Belief"* stated: "From the beginning of human civilization priests and 'holy men' have invented pious nonsense. For the priesthood the rewards have been immense: power, prestige and wealth. They have fused with, and become part of, the ruling elite. But times of social stress have always seen the emergence of a counter-priesthood, radicals or fundamentalists, preaching a purity of fable; ascetics, puritans and fanatics who revile and castigate a corrupt and worldly religious establishment and offer themselves as apostles of Truth and Divine Wisdom.

Rome's 1st century colonisation and exploitation of Judaea placed huge stresses on a theocracy that had enjoyed absolute power under the Maccabean kings and had been placated and indulged even by Herod the Great. Pharisees on the one hand – rabbinic guardians of a religious correctness, not part of the Temple hierarchy– and Essenes on the other – egalitarian purists, who withdrew to their own communities and lived by their own rule – trained the cadres, and fashioned the earliest ideology, for a radical recasting of Judaism. A century of endemic rebellion, civil war, and wars of national resistance, leading ultimately to catastrophic defeat, made ready the seed bed for a violent and profound religious revolution."----

In modern times however Christianity have reformed and become more tolerant religion, Christians are ready to listen and ready to reform and correct errors, but, the problems with Islam remains as it is, even in 21st century Islamists remain stubborn unwilling to relent and reform, not interested in adopting more progressive methods of life, Islam still believes in violence means to solve most of their problems, "Beheading, stoning woman to death, female genital cutting, man beating his wife, killing daughter or sister for family honour," such social ills still persists in Islam.

The problem with extremism is that no extremist force or an individual person will ever publicly agree and admit that they are extremists and believe in violence and suppression and that their community members and leaders are oppressors. Every social class and political class blames each other for increase in terrorism and deteriorating natural environment and global warming, "Conservatives blames the Liberals, Rightists elements blames the Leftists, Socialists blames Capitalists, Capitalists blames the Communists, Communists blames Zionists, Christianity blames Jewish and Judaism blames Islam and Islam blames all of the above," despite evident of Sunni Islamic folks responsible for so many barbaric crimes, killings and massacres yet Sunni Muslims pleads their innocence.

Who are terrorists? What is terrorism? This may be simple questions to ask, perhaps some people may conveniently answer such questions, but, **terrorism** is not a simple dictionary word that you simply open a book and find a meaning of it, terrorism has a very deeper meaning and there is lot to understand from many different perspective.

Here couple of pressing questions comes to mind of many; how and for what types of perpetrated crimes should the people belonging to particular ethnic or religious community can be branded and termed as terrorists? How to determine, as to, who are terrorists in real terms? Can we or is it possible to define terrorism? Otherwise the answer is simple > terrorists are those people who kills and traumatizes innocent people and causes destruction to businesses and properties, but opinions are divided large section of society argues that they are not terrorists but freedom fighters and fighting for humble cause and helping their ethnic or religious community, some say it is struggle for social justice, hence one section of society calls people indulging in brutal and senseless violence as terrorists and criminals, while another section of society defends the allege perpetrators and blames rival religious communities or particular country's government for tarnishing their community's image and thereby terms terrorists as revolutionary warriors.

It is because there are diverse interest and so many opposing and conflicting views and opinions, one large section of society calls people belonging to particular religious community indulging in violent and destructive activities as terrorists and criminals, but another minority yet significantly important section of society believes they are not terrorists but warriors and revolutionists freedom fighters and are fighting for the right cause and for social justice for the benefit of their ethnic or religious community or for the basic civil rights of poor and downtrodden.

Radicalizing people of particular ethnic or religious community is not actually work of politicians or religious leaders, it is the naïve and gullible people purposefully allows political extremist leaders or ethnic and religious community chieftains to brainwash them, large section in our society mindless people with utmost interest listens to and solemnly believes every illogical nonsense and rubbish these political extremists and self-seeking religious leaders speaks.

Toxic speeches delivered by hate-mongers only precipitates irrational hostile feelings among people, and that's when people belonging to a particular community starts disliking people of another particular rival ethnic or religious community or communities, this is, what is called **divide and rule**, when politicians and religious community hierarchy and chieftains instead of playing role of uniting people contrary to that plays destructive role of dividing people, spreads fear and creates sense of insecurity among people, and highly brainwashed gullible people makes all the wrong choices and are responsible for giving Political, financial and muscle power to all the wrong people, it is not the politicians or supreme head of any particular religious community who exploits people, it actually is/are large percentage of naïve and reckless common-people who allows opportunists forces and selfish elements to exploit them, therefore this is how corrupt people obtains economic and political power.

"Politicians are not fool, it is those foolish People who again and again keeps voting for the same Political parties and keep electing same politicians."

Not only does the politicians and religious hierarchy that take advantage of unprincipled and mindless people, but Movie stars, sports-personalities as well exploits people's sentiments by playing emotive card, if one large religious community is critical of a particular movie star and accuses and curses him/her of inappropriate behaviour or of corrupt practices, then another community to which the alleged movie star or sportsperson belongs to will sympathize and empathize and whole-heartedly support movie actor or actress who belongs to their own community. This is how crafty individual professional sports personalities and artists plays with the emotional feelings and succeed in mobilizing support for themselves and become successful in life and earn oodles of money and enjoys power of wealth and fame.

Therefore even <u>United Nation Security Council</u> have so far failed to define, as to, who should actually be called terrorists? Unable to decide parameters to judge and declare a particular group or organization of flouting rules and harming humanity for their own selfish interest.

For example, the same alleged jihadist folks in Afghanistan in 1980s who were fighting ferocious war against occupying <u>soviet army</u> were respectfully called Mujahideen (Holy-warrior, guerrilla fighters), but the Russians and their allies and the then Afghan government use to call these mujahideens as Terrorists, while the western countries as well as Sunni ruled Islamic countries use to call the Mujahideens as holy-warriors and saviours of Islam and humanity, but then when in 1990s when the same Mujahideens allegedly formed jihadists organization like "Taliban and Al Qaeda," and when **Osama bin laden** emphatically challenged entire world's non-Sunni Muslim communities and categorically stated that his Al Qaeda group has been formed to destroy everything that is against the ethics and principle of Sunni-Islam, and his Al Qaeda members are **Sacred Holy-Warriors** (Islamic army) and his jihadists are determined to obliterate western civilization, Osama Laden categorically stated his Islamic army won't rest till the time they've achieved their objective to establish **Islamic caliphate** all over the world. So the same people who were once friends and allies of America and other west-European countries now became one of their fiercest enemy, America a super-power country not ready to be pressurized, the than U.S. president "<u>George W Bush</u>" on his part vowing before people his nation and said in 2001 that America would hunt its enemies dismantle and degrade Sunni-Muslim terrorism and the terror network.

So, when it suits your purpose you justify activities of people indulging in abrupt and unlawful activities and call the violent activists as freedom fighters, and if is not to your convenience and if it is to your disadvantage then you brand people resorting to violent means of protest as criminals and terrorists.

To understand root cause of 21st century terrorism especially Sunni Islamic terrorism, we need to touch base with extreme ground realities, it all started when in 1979 the erstwhile **USSR** or to say Soviet Union forces invaded Afghanistan, while a small section of leftist leaning Afghanis welcomed soviet forces invasion but large majority population opposed Soviet invasion, we must also remember that was an era of **Cold-war** between the communist and socialist USSR and capitalist U.S.A and its western allies, hence the Americans as well were severely opposed because they disliked their arch rival Russia (a major constituent of USSR) occupying impoverished but strategically located Afghanistan, so those warlords and political parties fiercely opposed to Soviet invasion inside Afghanistan formed an alliance and were called **Mujahideen**, and these Mujahideens (guerrilla fighters) were openly aided and supported both financially and militarily by Pakistani and U.S. intelligence agency the **CIA**, large amount of funds, arms and ammunition as well as combative and strategic planning and explosive training was provided to the Mujahideens (guerrilla fighters) mainly by U.S. and also by rich Sunni-Arab countries.

Article title **"Why Did the Soviet Union Invade Afghanistan in 1979?"** Explains the reason; "The near seventy-year history of the Soviet Union is one dominated by its tradition of foreign military interventions that spanned most of its existence and stretched geographically from Krakow to the Kuril Islands. Within this trajectory, the Soviet invasion of, and subsequent war with Afghanistan (1979-1989) stands out in particular, as a lasting legacy of the Cold War. Globally, its outcome continues to plague international society in the current struggle between the Western liberal democratic order and Islamic extremism. Domestically, the remains of the war have rendered the nation's political institutions, economy and society fragile, and transformed Afghanistan into a battlefield for factional rivalries and a breeding ground for religious fundamentalism.

The invasion of Afghanistan was the Soviet Union's final foreign military intervention before its eventual dissolution in 1991. Soviet troops invaded Kabul on December 25th 1979, on order from Moscow to replace the radical Hafizullah Amin with the Soviet-endorsed Babrak Karmal as head of the Democratic Republic of Afghanistan. On December 31st, the Politburo announced, that by overthrowing Amin, they would ease the pace of Afghanistan's communist revolution and thereby protect the communist (PDPA) regime from collapsing due to its domestic unpopularity, and thereby ceding to Islamist and Western forces. Although in hindsight this provides the justification surrounding Moscow's decision, it gives little consideration of the concerns that drove the USSR to invade. Expanding upon those factors central to Soviet decision-making in 1979, this essay will argue that the Soviet decision to invade Afghanistan was foremost driven by the security concerns a rapidly weakening Afghanistan, vulnerable to Islamic extremism and Western encroachment, posed to the Soviet Union's southern borders. As the attempts at negotiation and sending advisors had failed to stabilise the PDPA regime from collapse, and consequently facing an increasingly narrowing set of options, military intervention became the favoured alternative. Facilitating this decision was the threat of the 'reversibility of communism' pervading across fragile Third World socialist states like South Yemen, Ethiopia and Angola; the pressures imposed by the Ustinov-Gromyko-Andropov troika in Politburo decision-making, heightened by reports by on-ground Soviet staff and advisors who were increasingly involved in Afghan affairs; and the end of Détente framework following the rejection of the SALT II Agreement by the United States Congress."…………

However, as the Soviet occupation dragged on, the Afghan resistance improved its internal cooperation. By 1985, the majority of mujahideen fought under a broad network or alliance called the Islamic Unity of Afghanistan Mujahideen. This alliance was made up of the troops from seven major warlords' armies, so it was also known as the Seven Party Mujahideen Alliance or the Peshawar Seven.

The most famous (and likely most effective) of the mujahideen commanders was **Ahmed Shah Massoud**, known as the "Lion of the Panjshir." His troops fought under the banner of the Jamiat-i-Islami, one of the Peshawar Seven factions led by Burhanuddin Rabbani, who would later become the 10th President of Afghanistan.

Massoud was a strategic and tactical genius, and his mujahideen were key to the Afghan resistance against the Soviet Union throughout the 1980s.

Foreign governments also supported the mujahideen in the **war against the Soviets**, for a variety of reasons. The United States had been engaged in detente with the Soviets, but this new expansionist move angered President Jimmy Carter, and the US would go on to supply money and arms to the mujahideen through intermediaries in **Pakistan** throughout the conflict. (The US was still smarting from its loss in the **Vietnam War**, so did not send in any combat troops.) The People's Republic of **China** also supported the mujahideen, as did **Saudi Arabia**.

The Afghani mujahideen deserve the lion's share of credit for their victory over the Red Army, however. Armed with their knowledge of the mountainous terrain, their tenacity, and their sheer unwillingness to allow a foreign army to over-run Afghanistan, small bands of often ill-equipped mujahideen fought one of the world's superpowers to a draw. In 1989, the Soviets were forced to withdraw in disgrace, having lost 15,000 troops plus 500,000 injured.

For the Soviets, it was a very costly mistake. Some historians cite the expense and discontent over the Afghan War as a major factor in the collapse of the Soviet Union several years later.

Bin Laden himself once said ``the collapse of the Soviet Union ... goes to God and the Mujahideen in Afghanistan ... the US had no mentionable role,'' but ``collapse made the US more haughty and arrogant.'9

Terrorism has in 21st century unofficially become an industry, many adventurous youngsters join terrorists groups or criminal gangs because they feel and see tremendous career opportunities, therefore they do not hesitate taking higher risk all for the sake of earning quick money and for extravagant lifestyle.

Rise in defence expenditure, but drop in earnings due to decline in economic activity therefore lower tax revenue, some of the war-torn and those countries affected by civil war there problems are intense and chronic, those countries whose economy mostly dependent on single source of income which is exporting petroleum oil & gas largely situated in North-Africa and west-Asia their governments have to increase local duties and taxes or have to borrow money from international financial institution or rely on mercy of donor nations, while it's a severe economic pain for common-people living in war-zones, it is moment of glory for many others, because unending wars and conflicts in countries also opens up business opportunities for many large Multinational companies, the demand for arms and ammunition, food and medicines increases, manufacturing and trading companies and power-brokers, military hardware and arms dealers, human traffickers and agents exploits the situation and gains a lot, makes vast amount of money.

India and Saudi Arabia are two of the most prolific arms importers, but other Asian countries such as Pakistan, Iraq and Iran as well are compel to increase defence spending, countries buying more arms, amination and other military hardware, not only countries but terrorists groups as well needs to buy sophisticated arms of course for their terror related activities, all this buying of defence equipment is unbelievably profitable for arms manufacturing and exporting industries, wars and conflicts and increase terrorism saves jobs as well creates more high paying skilled jobs in defence sector, arms and defence equipment manufacturers in U.S.A., France, Britain and Russia makes colossal profit.

Who funds whom? Who pays the bills? How are various terrorist groups and criminal gangs funded? First thing we need to understand is that no terrorist group and mafias or criminal gangs can survive unless they have political protection, support of politicians and influential military commanders is utmost necessary for any group or organization to carry-out terrorist activities in that particular country or region where they want to operate, also it is important for terrorist group to win support of at least one of the ethnic or religious community. So without the support of dominant ethnic or religious community and political patronage no terrorist group can ever survive.

Article title "**State Sponsored Terrorism: Terrorism Research**" explains; "Is there a difference between terrorism and the use of specific tactics that exploit fear and terror by authorities normally considered "legitimate"? Nations and states often resort to violence to influence segments of their population, or rely on coercive aspects of state institutions. Just like the idea of equating any act of military force with terrorism described above, there are those who equate any use of government power or authority versus any part of the population as terrorism. This view also blurs the lines of what is and is not terrorism, as it elevates outcomes over intentions. Suppression of a riot by law enforcement personnel may in fact expose some of the population (the rioters) to violence and fear, but with the intent to protect the larger civil order. On the other hand, abuse of the prerogative of legitimized violence by the authorities is a crime.

But there are times when national governments will become involved in terrorism, or utilize terror to accomplish the objectives of governments or individual rulers. Most often, terrorism is equated with "non-state actors", or groups that are not responsible to a sovereign government. However, internal security forces can use terror to aid in repressing dissent, and intelligence or military organizations perform acts of terror designed to further a state's policy or diplomatic efforts abroad.

A government that is an adversary of the United States may apply terror tactics and terrorism in an effort to add depth to their engagement of U.S. forces. Repression through terror of the indigenous population would take place to prevent internal dissent and insurrection that the U.S. might exploit. Military special operations assets and state intelligence operatives could conduct terrorist / extremist operations against U.S. interests both in theater and as far abroad as their capabilities allow. Finally, attacks against the U.S. homeland could be executed by state sponsored terrorist organizations or by paid domestic proxies. **Three different ways that states can engage in the use of terror are**:

• Governmental or "State" terror • State involvement in terror • State sponsorship of terrorism and extremism.

Governmental or "State" terror: Sometimes referred to as "terror from above", where a government terrorizes its own population to control or repress them. These actions usually constitute the acknowledged policy of the government, and make use of official institutions such as the judiciary, police, military, and other government agencies. Changes to legal codes permit or encourage torture, killing, or property destruction in pursuit of government policy. After assuming power, official Nazi policy was aimed at the deliberate destruction of "state enemies" and the resulting intimidation of the rest of the population. Stalin's "purges" of the 1930s are examples of using the machinery of the state to terrorize a population. The methods he used included such actions as rigged show trials of opponents, punishing family or friends of suspected enemies of the regime, and extra-legal use of police or military force against the population.

Saddam Hussein used chemical weapons on his own Kurdish population without any particular change or expansion of policies regarding the use of force on his own citizens. They were simply used in an act of governmental terror believed to be expedient in accomplishing his goals.

State involvement in terror: These are activities where government personnel carry out operations using terror tactics. These activities may be directed against other nations' interests, its own population, or private groups or individuals viewed as dangerous to the state. In many cases, these activities are terrorism under official sanction, although such authorization is rarely acknowledged openly. Historical examples include the Soviet and Iranian assassination campaigns against dissidents who had fled abroad, and Libyan and North Korean intelligence operatives downing airliners on international flights.

Another type of these activities is "death squads" or "war veterans": unofficial actions taken by officials or functionaries of a regime (such as members of police or intelligence organizations) against their own population to repress or intimidate. While these officials will not claim such activities, and disguise their participation, it is often made clear that they are acting for the state. Keeping such activities "unofficial" permits the authorities deniability and avoids the necessity of changing legal and judicial processes to justify oppression. This is different than "pro-state" terror, which is conducted by groups or persons with no official standing and without official encouragement. While pro-state terror may result in positive outcomes for the authorities, their employment of criminal methods and lack of official standing can result in disavowal and punishment of the terrorists, depending on the morality of the regime in question."……………..

Again the same question arises; Does "Petro-dollars" funds Islamic terrorism and extremism? Western media and politicians for decades have been complaining that the wealthy oil rich Sunni Arab countries such as Saudi Arabia, Qatar and Kuwait have been promoting and generously funding Islamic extremism and terrorism, so it is alleged that several prominent Muslim countries governments have been helping and promoting jihadist (Islamic holy-warriors) groups. It maybe be perception of many but perhaps not a reality. Perhaps, I would say its partially true that couple of Sunni Arab countries earning large amount of money selling petroleum oil & gas uses some amount of the oil income to fund Islamic extremism and terrorism, but as it is that no criminal gang or terrorist group can possibly sustain itself unless they've political patronage and until such time that they enjoy support of particular dominant ethnic or religious community. Therefore Sunni jihadist terrorism can't survive for a moment more unless they are backed and aided by their community members, clerics and political leaders.

There is a perception, and also true, can't deny the fact that there is **State sponsor terrorism**, wherein government of particular country for strategic reasons and for larger interest and benefit of their country they do finance extremist and terrorist groups, but it is equally true the other way around as well, which is that many criminal gangs and terrorist groups as well supports States by providing financial and other material help to governments and contributes significant amount of money for the welfare of people belonging to their own religious community.

Terrorism have been institutionalized, criminal syndicates and cartels as well as terrorist groups mobilize resources and finances from many different ways and means, Crime and Corruption have unofficially gained Industry Status. So talking about Islamic extremism and terrorism, Islamic terror and criminal enterprises, gangs and syndicates earns money and generates cash from many different means and are in position to fund governments and give big political donations to influential political leaders and political parties.

Sunni jihadist groups like "ISIS, Al Qaeda, Al Shabaab, Boko Haram," and many more fringe terror groups are allegedly involved in many illicit business and trade, while Africa based terror groups like Al Shabaab and Boko Haram, earns big amount of money to fund their jihadist project mainly through Poaching and killing wildlife in African forest and jungles and trade in endanger animals skins, bones and ivory, also earns money from illegal mining of minerals and extortion, seeking donations forcing people to donate money for Islamic causes which obviously is for jihad (Islam holy-war).

Similarly other terrorist groups like ISIS, Al Qaeda and Taliban and other criminal gangs mostly operating in west-Asia's Arabian countries, Afghanistan and Pakistan are allegedly involve in many unlawful and illegal business and trade such as "human trafficking, drug trafficking, trafficking in human organs, fake currency, counterfeit medicines, cybercrime, gambling and illegal betting and match fixing." So reverse is true as well with hundreds of billions of dollars they earn from all kinds of illicit and illegal business and trade, many of the criminal gangs and terrorist groups finance and funds also bribes the governments and government officials of many countries.

With trillions of dollar of expenditure incurred for fighting wars and fighting against the terrorists and insurgent armies in various Islamic countries in Asia and Africa, some more individual people and corporates may have profited, yes, indeed, the defence contractors, arms dealers, arms and ammunition manufacturing companies and defence equipment suppliers have all made oodles of money, not to forget corrupt politicians and government officials in several Islamic countries affected by terrorism and civil wars as well have immensely benefited. It was initially said before the start of war on terror, that, this war on terror is to serve Human Purpose, but as things have unravel, the facts began to surface, it has become evident that the war on terror has actually served and fulfilled purpose of egocentric self-seeking individuals and businessmen and above all served Commercial Interest.

With regards to U.S spending Trillions of Dollars on War on Terror, instead U.S government officials and ruling administration would had been better advised had U.S instead of spending Trillions fighting wars in Iraq and Afghanistan and then expanding war on terror to other Islamic countries in the Persian gulf region, had U.S used this trillions of dollars at home on repairing and upgrading existing infrastructure and developing new infrastructure and used money on providing healthcare benefits to its citizens, all these expenditure would have helped create millions of jobs in all of north-America and would have helped accelerate growth of domestic industry in U.S.

There is a famous saying "Politics makes strange bedfellows," politicians also have brazen double standards, America's staunchest ally in the west-Asia is none other than Saudi Arabia, now Americans and European politicians and intellectual class talks a lot and delivers emotional speeches condemning human rights abuses and favours freedom of speech and civil liberties, and pleads for social justice for all, but strangely enough U.S strongest ally the Saudis are arguably the worst human rights abuser with brutal track record of suppression of its citizens particularly targeting minorities and women.

Not only that Saudi Arabia is ferocious offender of human rights, but is also responsible for committing genocide inside its neighbouring impoverish country **Yemen**, Saudi is one of the world's leading importer of arms and ammunitions, Saudi purchases most of its military hardware and ammunitions from Britain, U.S. and perhaps also from France, Saudi army ostensibly has been using British made weapons to target Shia Houthis inside Yemen and according to some estimates Saudi Arabia's army between 2014/15 is responsible for killing 6,000 Shias most of those killed are/were civilians in Yemen, flouting all international convention and rules, while Saudi Arabia is committing barbaric war crimes killing mainly civilian population and destroying infrastructure and properties worth hundreds of millions dollar, and the greatest advocates of human rights and social justice, the French, British and Germans are merely staring at events happening inside Yemen, maintaining stoic silence not a word of condemnation or expression of solidarity with Shia community, Sunni Islamic folks supresses the minority Shia community and western countries disgracefully ignores cruel atrocities committed against Shiite population.

Not just the Saudis but another devout western ally the Israelis as well are doing there bit to allegedly help the Sunni jihadists, Israel often targets key Shiite army bases and installation in Syria and Lebanon to allegedly help Sunni insurgent jihadi army consolidate their position inside Syria, also it has been reported as well has been witnessed that many of the seriously injured and wounded Al Qaeda and Al Nusra front terrorists when they suffer injuries or are wounded many of these wounded jihadists allegedly receives medical care and treatment in Israeli hospitals.

With regards to Syrian civil war, it is alleged that initially at the start of civil war in Syria in 2011/12 many incidents of killing innocent civilians and massacres were strategically planned and committed by pro-western and Saudi backed jihadists and systematically blamed pro government Syrian army for all the killings to defame and to denigrate secular Syrian president Bashar al-Assad.

Hot rhetoric but soft action, we see and listen American, French, British and many other countries politicians delivering aggressive hard hitting speeches against the so-called Radical Islamist jihadists, and in strongly worded language **vows** and **pledges** before their people that they'll not rest until the moment they destroy Sunni Islamic terror network and decimate jihadi terrorism, well, this are all talk, **War on terror** --- on ground there is very little action mere academic or to say un-pragmatic fight against Sunni terrorism, be it in Afghanistan, Iraq or Syria, western army action is over-reported in media while in real term very little happens on the battle ground. Prominent Sunni jihadi forces are or have gained immense strength and No western army or any other significantly strong armed forces are sincerely trying to stop the menace of Islamic terror, no one daring to hunt them out and destroy Sunni terrorist groups who are spread in so many different parts of Asia and in Africa, Somalia based Al – Shabaab incredibly powerful terrorist outfit in east-Africa, Nigeria based Boko Haram arguably the most dreaded terrorist group, besides Nigeria Boko Haram terrorists terrorizes in many other countries in west and central Africa, Afghanistan based Radical Sunni terrorist group Taliban has become more stronger than it ever was between 2012 and 2015, so apart from *ISIS and Al Qaeda* there are many Sunni terrorist groups who are ferociously and frivolously carrying out terrorist activities, unrestrictedly terrorizing and humiliating innocent civilians, but no army or security forces *"worth its salt"* have genuinely attempted to eliminate these terrorists organizations, Boko Haram, Al Shabaab or Taliban remains largely untouched and unchallenged.

Evidently it is only the Iranian backed Shiite army and other Shiite groups like Shia-Houthis and Hezbollah's army are seen fighting Sunni jihadist terrorists in Iraq, Syria and even in Yemen.

According to historians, it was in June-632AD immediately after the death of the founder of Islam Prophet Mohammed, it is believed Islam got divided into two faction "**Shia and Sunni**," now as per my own understanding about Islamic history, it is for the first time in hundreds of years since Islam got divided into two faction that the Shiites have grouped themselves and they are resolutely opposing Sunnis highhandedness and vehemently fighting against Sunni terrorism, or else for all these hundreds of years the Sunnis have dominated and have brutally suppressed and battered the beleaguered Shia community.

The dynamics of Middle-East conflict changed and all new dimension was added to Islamic sectarian war in west-Asia when the Russian armed forces threw their weight behind Syrian and Shiite army, long after observing war from safer distance, the Russian army stepped in and completely changed the complexion of war in Arabian countries, sometime in middle of year 2015 the audacious and assiduous incumbent Russian President Vladimir Putin ordered his Airforce commanders to bombard the Sunni terrorists hideouts and camps inside Syria. Russian forces mainly targeting Western and Saudis and Qataris backed jihadists camps, Russia's military response thoroughly irked the western power, the *French, British and Americans* shocked and flabbergast with Russian Airforce action largely targeting jihadist the so-called free Syrian army whom the western power had long been nurturing, training and aiding to fight against Iranian backed army to gain control in the petroleum oil and gas rich west-Asia region, western allies in the west-Asia region Sunni power Saudi Arabia and Turkey as well were jittery and tense by Russian president Putin's bold initiatives and rendering his support to their arch rival and known foe the Shiite army.

"Russia's support for Syria dates back to 1946, when Russia helped consolidate Syria's independence. The two countries mutually came to a diplomatic and military agreement in the form of a non-aggression pact, which was enacted on April 20, 1950. In this pact, Russia promised support to the newly-created Syria by helping to develop its military and by providing tactical support. Essentially, Russia and Syria have been cooperating for decades both militarily and economically, with Russia maintaining a naval base on the Syrian Mediterranean."

Russia's increasingly aggressive posture has sparked a sweeping review among U.S. defence strategists of America's military policies and contingency plans in the event of a conflict with the former Soviet state. With the launch of airstrikes in Syria, Russian President Vladimir Putin instigated a proxy war with the U.S., putting those nation's powerful militaries in support of opposing sides of the multipolar conflict. And it's a huge gamble for Moscow.

Here to have a better perspective of the two main political and economic system **Capitalism** and **Socialism** which are principle system that most of the countries across the world use or have adopted to govern their respective country, I would like to share excerpts from article "**Capitalism & Socialism: Two Old Economic Visions**" Theories, we are often told, are merely abstractions with no real practical impact, but hardly anything has impacted modern history more profoundly than capitalism and socialism. ~ Riane Eisler, The Real Wealth of Nations

For most of recorded history, whether Eastern or Western, the vast majority of people were poor, and, as they had been taught to do, accepted poverty as their inevitable lot. But as the industrial revolution gained steam in Europe, so did the possibility that the world can change. By the middle 1700s, the vision of progress through human intervention was applied to economics. If people could improve the means of production, perhaps they could also improve the economic system. With a better understanding of how economic systems function, we could make them work for the greater good of all.

Out of this new probing of economic patterns, two economic theories emerged. The first theory described what we today call capitalism. The second theory is what its proponents called socialism.

Theories, we are often told, are merely abstractions with no real practical impact, but hardly anything has impacted modern history more profoundly than capitalism and socialism. Understanding these theories and the times out of which they came is key to recognizing the dominator assumptions embedded in them, and to building a new economic theory called *partnerism* – one that really works for the greater good of all.

The Capitalist Vision

Adam Smith (born in Scotland in 1723) wrote his famous *Inquiry into the Nature and Cases of the Wealth of Nations* in 1776, the same year the United States was born. Smith's book, better known simply as *The Wealth of Nations*, became the "bible" of capitalist theory. Smith's was an optimistic vision of the future. He basically accepted the dominator belief that people are inherently selfish. But in his view, this selfishness could work for the common good – if only the market was left to regulate production and commerce without government interference.

Smith wrote in a time of massive social and economic dislocation. The gentry had appropriated most of the lands that were commons, and hordes of dispossessed farmers reduced to paupers were roaming the countryside. There were also already signs of what was to come with the advent of full-fledged 19th century industrialization. In some places, young children worked in mines 12 hours a day as did women, including pregnant women, who sometimes gave birth in mine shafts. Conditions in some manufacturing towns weren't much better, with children tending machines round the clock for twelve to fourteen hours at a stretch.

The Socialist Vision

In important respects, capitalism was a step forward in the move from a dominator to a partnership way of life. It gave impetus to more socially accountable political forms, such as constitutional monarchies and republics, and was a major factor in the creation of a middle class. Certainly capitalism was preferable to the earlier feudal and mercantile economic systems in which nobles and kings owned most economic resources.

However, capitalism emphasized individual acquisitiveness and greed (the profit motive), relied on rankings (the class structure), continued traditions of violence (colonial conquests and wars), and failed to recognize the economic importance of the "women's work" of caring and caregiving. In these and other ways, capitalism retained significant dominator elements.

By the 19th century, when it was clear that capitalism was not fulfilling Smith's vision of an economics that works for the common good, Karl Marx and Friedrich Engels proposed a very different theory. Theirs was to be known as scientific socialism, and it challenged just about everything Smith had believed – particularly his faith in the forces of the market.

Marx's and Engels' scientific socialism was an alternative to what they dismissed as the utopian socialism of theorists such as Robert Owen and Charles Fourier. Marx and Engels believed that class conflicts are historically inevitable, and that the victory of the bourgeoisie or merchant class over the feudal landed aristocracy would inevitably be followed by the victory of the working class or proletariat. But they were not only committed to constructing a new economic theory; they were also committed to seeing it put into action.

In time, Marx's and Engels' dream of a successful communist revolution was realized. But not in an industrialized capitalist nation, as they had predicted. Instead, revolution came in an agricultural semi-feudal society: the Russia of autocratic tsars and nobles.

Although socialist policies ended mass hunger and destitution and vastly improved healthcare and education, traditions of domination in both the family and state did not change. What Marx called the dictatorship of the proletariat turned into just that – another violent and despotic regime.

The central planners created a top-down form of state capitalism where resources were controlled by a small group of men from the top. In Moscow, government apparatniks got perks such as seaside villas and sumptuous banquets, while the mass of people lived in overcrowded flats and often lacked staple foods. In the provinces, warlords became communist commissars and continued to terrorize their people.

Part of the problem lay in communist theory itself. Not only did it dictate the abolition of private property and class warfare; it also failed to abandon the dominator tenet that violence is the means to power, as in the well-known adage "The end justifies the means." But an even bigger part of the problem was the rigid dominator nature of the culture that preceded the Soviet Union.".................

Islamic terrorism and extremism is more flamboyant and candid, hence it is easily recognizable, but there are extremist and self-radicalized individual people in other communities as well, like for example there are extremist and self-radicalized Hindus as well, unlike Islamist terrorists the Hindu terrorism and extremism is more subtle and discreet. Overall the problem with extremism is that no extremist ever is ready to admit or to agree he/she is an extremist, each extremist person have a tendency to plead innocence and to gain sympathy from others.

Talking about Hindu extremism, as Hinduism is majority religion in India, the right wing Hindu political party takes considerable advantage of islamophobia and hate preacher Hindu leaders brainwash naïve and gullible section of Hindu community, and the big section of senseless Hindus believes every nonsense talks of Hindu political leaders and recklessly sympathizes and votes for the Hindus political party, this is how right wing Hindu political party in India wins elections by instilling fears of Islamic terrorism in the minds of Hindu population, Hindu extremist groups always systematically defame Islam by falsely implicating and blaming the Muslims for perpetrated crimes even if those crimes aren't committed by Muslims. So this type of politics is called *divide and rule*. The mainstream media in India is incompetent and inept and largely controlled by fundamentalist Hindu business houses, therefore bias and prejudice media helps causes of right wing Hindu political party by propagating pro-Hindu propaganda.

If we talk of bigger issues in global politics, America being dominant player in international business and political affairs, hence globally those people who are interested in politics and economics takes keen interest in U.S.A's domestic economic and political policies as well as focuses on U.S role in international politics, because U.S is world's largest economy and strongest possible military power in the world, America is often criticize for its foreign policies. For those who study foreign affairs and have been tracking U.S foreign policies will know that U.S foreign policies often harms U.S and more so to the Americans, whether it was U.S involvement in Chinese domestic affairs in the 1930s during Japanese aggression in China, or U.S.A's involvement and indulgence in Korean and Vietnam civil wars was a total fiasco, and of course U.S role in West-Asia and Persian gulf countries internal politics and religious affairs and dealing with Islamic rulers has always been troublesome.

U.S politicians over indulges in Islamic affairs and senselessly involve itself or by default gets involve in Muslim countries civil wars and Islamic internal problems, it is time that U.S. politicians and government administrative officers withdraw themselves from domestic problems of Muslim countries and distance themselves from Islamic religious wars, better leave it to the Muslims to sort out Islamic troubles and let the Arabs and Persians sort out their differences in which so ever possible manner,

It will be better that U.S maintains safe distance from all other regions conflict zones, not just away from Islamic countries but even keep itself away from South-China sea troubles, North-Korea developing nuclear weapons, north-Korea testing Hydrogen Nuclear Bomb and threatening U.S of dire consequences if U.S interferes in Korean matters and if it helps north-Korea's unfriendly neighbouring countries, let the Arabs sought out Islamic problems, Japanese, Koreans and Chinese will sought out their territorial disputes, U.S trying to play dominant role in international affairs is only endangering its own sovereignty and risking life of its own citizens.

It is thought to us that we learn from our past mistakes and never repeat the same mistakes again, but U.S.A didn't learn lesson from Vietnam fiasco, the then U.S. President **Mr George W Bush** in aftermath of 9/11 terror attacks on U.S soil, ordered his army to first attack Afghanistan in 2001 and later invaded Iraq to dislodge from power the brutal Iraqi dictator Saddam, it proved to be a miscalculated move, and created even bigger political and financial mess than Vietnam and Korea had proved to be, it sometime takes time for us to realize our mistakes, so did the Americans, after the loss of thousands of American soldiers lives and incurring Trillions of Dollars in expenses, a decade or so later the Americans started saying with regret that it was a wrong strategy and a grave strategic blunder for U.S.A to have got involve in Islamic war in Islamic countries, not only the socialists who either way were deeply sceptical about war on terror but even more hardliners the rightists elements in U.S. as well admit it would have been better if U.S.A had not got directly involved in military confrontation with Sunni terrorist army in Afghanistan and Iraq.

U.S politicians and government officials over involvement in overseas affairs has left little or no time it seems to solve ever increasing domestic problems, domestic troubles are mounting at alarming pace in U.S, if we take into account number of deaths in U.S by Islamic terrorists between 2002 and 2015, no more than couple of hundred Americans may have been killed by Sunni jihadists on U.S soil, but what U.S politicians and citizens needs to be more worried about and there only concern should be the brutal rise in killings of innocent Americans in Gun violence, according to estimates each year as many as 30,000 people in U.S.A dies or are killed in Gun violence and by their own home grown terrorists, apart from gun violence there's devastatingly high cases and incidents of racial and religious discrimination and even more troublesome is deteriorating climatic conditions hurricanes, tornados, floods, snow storms and drought. Gosh so much trouble inside U.S, you guys (American folks) in 21st century the U.S politicians better spend more time at home to sort out domestic problems.

So it is not just Islamic wars that world needs to be concern about there are more serious and devastatingly dangerous political issues and problems that threatens global peace and security. In an article **"How Potent are North Korea's threats? – in' BBC;"** has written "**North Korea's threats**

North Korea has frequently employed bellicose rhetoric towards its perceived enemies.

In 1994 South Koreans stocked up on essentials in panic after a threat by a North Korean negotiator to turn Seoul into "a sea of fire" - one which has been repeated several times since.

After US President George W Bush labelled it part of the "axis of evil" in 2002, Pyongyang said it would "mercilessly wipe out the aggressors".

In June 2012 the army warned that artillery was aimed at seven South Korean media groups and threatened a "merciless sacred war".

There is also a pattern of escalating threats whenever South Korea gets a new leader, with misogynist rhetoric directed at South Korea's first female President Park Geun-hye after she was elected in 2013.

While many observers dismiss the rhetoric as bluster, others warn of "the tyranny of low expectations" when it comes to understanding North Korea, because there have been a number of serious regional confrontations.

"If you follow North Korean media you constantly see bellicose language directed against the US and South Korea and occasionally Japan is thrown in there, and it's hard to know what to take seriously. But then when you look at occasions where something really did happen, such as the artillery attack on a South Korean island in 2010, you see there were very clear warnings," Professor John Delury at South Korea's Yonsei university told the BBC.

The North consistently warned that military exercises being conducted in the area would spark a retaliation.
Mr Delury argues that misreading Pyongyang's intentions and misunderstanding its capabilities has kept the US and South Korea **stuck in a North Korean quagmire.**

Picking apart the bluster

In recent years, the North has warned of a pre-emptive nuclear attack on the US in response to the prospect of joint military exercises between South Korea and the US.

"Any time a nation threatens pre-emptive nuclear war, there is cause for concern. North Korea is no exception, with its... shift in rhetoric from accusing the US of imagining a North Korean ballistic missile threat, to vowing to use its ballistic missile capabilities to strike the continental US," says Andrea Berger, from the Royal United Services Institute in London."...........

The U.S.A, French, Britain, and Germany's political leaders and government officials have for decades been busily involved in Persian gulf politics and kept themselves occupied with Islamic world's Islamic problems, overindulging in Muslim dominated countries civil wars and sorting out political and religious dispute, these progressive western countries have solved No problems but have created more problems in Islamic world.

So if the politicians have been involving themselves with Islamic affairs, the business community and also Banking and financial institutions top Executives of rich developed industrialized western countries as well the Japanese business houses have for decades since 1990s been taking keen interest in India's and China's business and economic prospect, the large Multinational corporates and financial institutions from industrialized countries like U.S, Britain, Germany and Japan have invested unprecedented amount of their time and money in India and China,

Over emphasis on growth prospect of India and China by the large Multinational companies and venture capitalists and over investing vast amount of money in these two world's most populous countries, and at the same time not bothering to look for commercial value and business opportunities in other parts of the world, there are many other countries apart from India and China which have significant economic potential yet brazenly been ignored by large multinational companies despite the fact many other countries as well are full of potential and offers excellent business opportunities and chance to make good amount of money.

There are many other promising countries with strong fundamentals, countries like **Iran** for example is land full of opportunities and have lot of scope to become 21st century economic powerhouse, other countries like Ethiopia and Indonesia have excellent business environment and best suited location to do business, then there are countries like Pakistan, Bangladesh and Philippine all these heavily populated countries with large younger demographic are full of potential and are best suited destinations for businesses ideal location for manufacturing and service sector, but there are two region of the world in particular which have lots of potential and have lots to offer to the world in terms of adding superlative value to global economic growth but sadly have been ignored for long time, here I'm talking about entire west-African block of countries and south-America (Latin America), both these region of the world have largely been neglected.

The American and British investment bankers and economists have been traveling to India to give advice to Indian government and corporates as in what measures should to be adopted and how economic and trade policy needs to be planned and implemented to attract foreign investments which will help spur India's economic growth, these economists and financial analysts as well as the merchant bankers and investment bankers instead of wasting their time and money advising Indians, they should have given some of their good advice and suggestions to the U.S government instead, because there are and were some best business and investment opportunities in U.S itself, Americans instead of looking for investment opportunities elsewhere and lecturing others how to grow their respective country's economy have missed out on some spectacular business and investment opportunities in their own country.

From 1995 until 2012 both India and China's economy were growing at steady pace, especially China's economic growth in superfast lane growing at significantly higher rate, but since 2013 China's fast pace economic growth hit a rough patch and considerably slowed down due to wide variety of reasons, emergence of newer low cost producing countries where products can be manufactured at much lower cost, so increase completion from other low cost manufacturers and also increase labour cost in China and factory workers imperious demand causing significant labour unrest, but there is another perspective for Chinese economic slowdown and much bigger problem which is/was climatic problems, as it is that as of 2015 China is world's biggest Greenhouse gas emitter, hence due to toxic air pollution China's government authority had to order many terrible air polluting industrial and manufacturing units to either suspend their production or close there industrial units all to gather. Since China's economic strength is in its manufacturing sector so any upheavals or problems that causes harm to manufacturing industries in China is or was bound to derail China's economic growth, so that's what happened in year 2014/15, also it is alleged that China's banking and financial sector is thoroughly disorganized and inefficient and that was one among many other reason for massive fall in China's stock-markets in 2nd half of 2015.

Similar is the story of economic slowdown in India, India's apparent economic strength was in offering low cost low-end back-office and customer service to overseas clients and customers, but less than satisfactory service of Indian companies and another reason being innovation and upgradation of new age modern technology, like for example Cloud computing technology and innovation of automated machines most of the work nowadays of providing service to customers is done or happens online or new age automated machines helps the customers, hence less manpower required, so in case of India as well emergence of competition from other countries and upgradation of technology has severely impacted India's economic growth prospect.

Another reason for India's economy not performing well is because of devastating slowdown in its agriculture sector, India primarily is agri-economy, India's strength once upon a time use to be its agriculture and farming sector, during 1970s and 1980s India's agriculture sector use to grow 7% to 9% annually, but since 2005 India's agriculture sector is performing much below expectation, and is in continuous slump, because of persistent slump in India's agriculture sector it is brutally harming approximately 55% of India's population who all fortunes are either directly or indirectly dependent on agriculture, the reason for declining agriculture sector in India is mostly because of extremely unpredictable weather pattern, there is either drought or extraordinarily excessive rain or unseasonal rains ruins much of the standing crops, so because of considerably large population of India have erratic monthly or annual income, because of economic uncertainty in millions of Indian household therefore consumption demand is not picking up as to the desire levels.

So as per some mathematical calculations both China and India may report that their respective country's GDP is growing at 7% or 8% annually, agree or disagree, but this GDP figures even if it's true perhaps it maybe but the reality is that this reported economic growth is not at all creating new high paying high quality jobs, leave alone talk about high paying even low skill jobs are hard to find in India and China for many of their citizens. And if there is talk about rebalancing and restructuring to transform their economy, when large percentage of your country's working age population are being made redundant or are unable to find new jobs, how than can we expect domestic consumption to rise, when people have no money in their pockets because they don't have suitable job.

Whether its manufacturing sector or services sector, in more competitive business environment, upgradation and innovation of new age technology, **cloud computing, smart-software, automated machines and robotic technology** helps businesses and industry become more efficient and productive and requires lot less staff.

Both the two most populous countries India and China aren't able to create enough job opportunities for their younger demographic, so because of lower business confidence and lack of job opportunities, plus high degree of uncertainty over future prospects all combinations of factors have considerably reduced purchasing power of Indians and Chinese. Therefore it was not surprising why demand for luxury items and expensive consumer products on high-street registered steep decline in the year 2015.

The swift pace of China's currency decline threatened to undermine global economic growth and exerted pressure on markets at a time when many countries particularly resource dependant countries like Russia, Brazil and Australia were already struggling. China's move to devalue its currency at best may be seen as distress signal from Beijing indicating to the rest of world that underlying fundamental of its economy were not that strong and are/were much weaker than it was believed to be. Swelling levels of debt, bloated state companies and an overall aversion to market forces are swamping China, threatening to derail its ascent to the ranks of rich countries. Faced with persisting drags on the economy—industrial overcapacity, an overbuilt property market and high corporate debt levels—the leadership has been trying to temper expectations by a public used to high rates of growth.

The bigger issue is in emerging market debt. Commodity focused corporates in Brazil, Russia, India and China that have borrowed in US dollars will face ruin next year (2016). The rising value of the US dollar and collapse of emerging market currencies will make repayments unaffordable for many. The collapse of the junk bond market will reach far and wide. In the past, the junk bond market has only really been used by professional investors or those with a higher risk appetite. As interest rates were cut from 2009 onwards retail investors, pension funds and insurance companies alike have all ploughed billions into high-yield bonds.

Western countries governments and institutional as well as retail investors felt the jolt, due to sharp devaluation of Russian, Indian and Chinese currency and falling stock-markets, due to China's weak economic data in first week of January-2016 itself China stock markets suffered unprecedented losses, massive fall resulted in U.S$2.5 Trillion erosion in market capitalization worldwide, which sent shock waves across global financial markets and all the leading stock markets across the world fell and saw steep decline in valuations. However exact quantum and amount of financial loss suffered has not been reported but it will be safe to assume that many Portfolio investors, Pension funds, hedge funds and investment banks of western countries particularly those from U.S and Britain and also Japanese who all had heavily invested in Indian and China stock markets and also had invested in debt instruments like government bonds have/had suffered monumental financial losses.

So it always makes sense to have well balanced business strategy and always nice to hedge risk, and to have mixed and diversify investment portfolio.

Now there is another perspective, during times when the large Western and Japanese Multinational companies and banks were overwhelmingly interested in India's and China's economic growth prospect and keen to invest money in India and China.

The Chinese made a smart move, China gradually and smartly started growing their trade and commerce with the African countries, also started making investment in Africa in a big way, in 1980 it seems the trade between China and Africa was only U.S$1 Billion, which spectacularly grew to over US$200 Billion by 2014.

Not just China started investing in Africa and increased its trade and commerce with African countries, but China also improved its ties with Latin American (south-America) countries, and have recoded magnificent growth in trade and commerce with Latin American countries, China trade with south-American countries is more than entire European continent countries put together.

The south-American region of the world has grossly been ignored by the rest of the world, not just Latin America offers excellent economic opportunities, but most people in the world don't know one more brutal fact about Latin America that it is arguably the most corrupt and violence prone region of the world. The mainstream western Media is fully focused on Islamic problems and terrorism, the violence and terrorist activities in Islamic countries is prominently reported and extensively covered by western media. The U.S and west-European politicians and government officials only have Arabian problems and India's and China's economic growth prospect on top of their mind, little or no time do these western politicians have to understand the tremendous business and economic growth prospect of Africa particularly west-Africa and more importantly the crimes that occurs in almost every south-American countries. Street corner shootouts, drug trafficking, mafias and criminal gang wars, apart there are rampant incidents of robbery, cheating, kidnappings and killings in south-American cities and countries.

So Latin America has both sides of it, the combination of good and bad, there is positive side of it and negative side of the reality, depends on you, how you perceive things, so ignoring the negative side, let us have positive perspective, we'll discuss **positive aspect** of south-America, South America has lot to offer in terms of business opportunities and lot to see and learn about their Great culture, wonderful people and its glorious history.

Latin America should be a fertile source of business opportunities. Latin America is not only geographically close to U.S but is rich in natural resources, has a relatively young population and possesses political institutions that are becoming increasingly democratic and stable. The conditions appear to be conducive for ample trade and international investment opportunities.

Latin America is made up of countries with commonalities in history and language but also remarkable differences in ethnic makeup, size and cultural traits. Differences also abound in the countries' levels of income and in their investment and commercial relationships with the U.S. and the rest of the world. Understanding these large differences—with the U.S. and among fellow Latin American countries—is vital to understanding the challenges and opportunities for the U.S. south of its border.

China has been seen as an alternative to the United States and Europe by Latin American nations for support in the international community, for funding of infrastructure and humanitarian aid, and for creating economic growth.

The Inter-American Development Bank says Latin America is the next global bread basket. With a third of the world's fresh water resources and more than a quarter of its good quality farmland, this region has everything China needs.

Latin America's trade with China will surpass that of the continent with Europe in two years, according to a United Nations study, with some predicting it will eventually eclipse its trade with the United States. Chinese investment in the continent's energy and infrastructure sectors is rising rapidly, with more than US$550 billion of infrastructure projects in the market.

China's growth in the past decade and its insatiable appetite for commodities has seen resource-rich countries like Brazil prosper. Latin America's largest economy is now the world's biggest exporter of foodstuffs like sugar cane, orange juice and soybean. Much of it is destined for Asia.

Some other reasons, why this world is ridden by poverty is because of structural discriminations and systematic bias, gender discrimination particularly against females, still living with primitive era mind-set, many ethnic and religious communities are yet reluctant to adopt modern norms and modern style of living, socially conservative religious communities do not allow their daughters the freedom to step out of there house and explore the world, explore to seize an opportunities to become career oriented, many fanatics in some religious communities do not allow their women and girls to make career in Singing, dancing acting, sports or to become fashion models, so as a result of which millions of girls outrageously remains in confinement of their house and under close observation of elder members of their community, so, this is how, many women and girls are deprived of the opportunities to manifest their charm and prove their abilities.

Language becomes another hurdle in progress of many youths, also, "**Linguistic chauvinism**" becomes stumbling-block in social and economic development of some countries. English is De facto a world's language, as, English is widely spoken and most preferred and understood language in the world, apart from English there are few other languages as well which are spoken and understood by more than Billion people around the world, languages like Hindi and Mandarin are couple of other most popular languages, while Hindi and Urdu language is spoken and understood in major parts of the Indian sub-continent and other Asian countries and Mandarin is a Chinese language spoken and understood by over billion people in China and other far eastern Asian countries, apart from these Three widely spoken languages there are other languages as well like French, Spanish and German which are as well considerably popular languages.

We learn to speak multiple languages perhaps not because we love that particular language/languages but we learn languages to connect with people from other parts of the world, for trade and commerce purpose, to understand different cultures and civilizations by communicating with people from different religions and regions of the world, but there apparently are folks in many countries from different communities and ethnic groups who are unrelenting, they do not like learning languages other than their own language (which they consider as their Mother tongue) as they fear that if they learn to speak English, Hindi or Mandarin or any other national languages in such case there young generation will stop communicating among themselves in their own language, hence their language which they relate it to their culture will lose identity. It is a "Strategic Blunder" on part of those who hold such linguistic prejudice because not learning multiple languages especially the dominating languages of the world which are spoken and understood by over billion people, most people seriously and comprehensively lose out on opportunities in life because one reason is that their own country perhaps may be debt ridden impoverish nation and may not provide good enough jobs and business opportunities and other reason because of Language Barrier they will always find it difficult to blend themselves with folks from other communities and countries.

Linguistic prejudice potentially holds back the progress and development of countries and their demographics.

The problems have been institutionalized, to eradicate poverty, we need globally coordinated approach, we need free market trade policies, **Chronic economic and humanitarian aid leads to Chronic problems**. The simple solution is to have more rational Liberal global trade policies, global commerce and trade policies needs to become more rational and unbiased, tariff structure needs to be restructured and be made more simpler with lower tariff and duties on items, easy availability of credit, no particular country should enjoy special privileges and each country should be at Par with other competing nations, so that it enables level playing field to all, Monopolies should be broken.

Frequent "Grants and financial aid packages" provided to the impoverish 3rd world and underdeveloped countries only further aggravates the situation, creates more uncertainty, because it makes governments and their people become more lethargic and loses fighting spirit to meet global challenges. There is no harm in taking or seeking help and support from others in dire circumstances once in a while, but, don't ever make it a habit to live and to survive on others help and support, because it makes a person/persons ever so dependent on others and he/she loses ability to do anything constructive on their own and forever remains dependant on others help and support.

What is urgently needed is to empower the youths and women, provide them access to necessary skills and training so that they become more independent and can manage themselves at work. What is most required, is large amount of money which needs to be allocated for the welfare and benefit of **Senior Citizens**, it is the elder senior citizens who need more care and special attention, so sincere support is required to develop old-age homes for the elders who are alone and suffers extreme health problems, therefore in each country, their government agencies should have volunteers to help safeguard the interest of senior citizens in every possible manner, in every aspect and respect.

Like Latin America another larger part of the world which is West-Africa, W-Africa also provides excellent business opportunities, good for almost every kind of businesses, Service sector, manufacturing sector and agriculture sector, plus affordable low cost labour, high scope to exploit minerals and setting up upstream manufacturing industries to make high-end value added products, large companies and businesses and venture capitalists needs to take risk of making investments in diverse fields and in different parts of the world, countries in Africa and south-America needs massive investments and need technological upgradation, it is needed for global peace and stability, there will be peace in our world only when we create jobs for youngsters,

It is always good to be politically correct, but when Politicians are politically incorrect, than "All hell breaks loose," something that happened in Greece, Greece might have glorious ancient history of gods and goddesses, according to some historians Greece is a birthplace of Western civilization, but 21st century Greek politicians are inept, insipid and ineffective at least that's what they've proved to be, Greece economy plunged into severe crisis sometime in 2010 and it was first sovereign debt crisis in the *Eurozone*, structural weakness, in Greek economy caused sudden crisis of confidence among lenders, in 2012 Greece government had largest **sovereign debt default** in history, and as of 2015 Greece's economy showing no sign of any significant recovering, Greece's citizens have been facing some brutal economic hardship, all because of flawed and faulty economic and political decisions taken by Greece's politicians and country's governing authority, at least on 2 occasions first in 2014 and later in 2015 there was an opportunity for Greece to exit from European union, break all ties with European union and to get rid of the diktat of ECB (*European central bank*) and of IMF (international monetary fund), but for reasons best known to the ruling political dispensation of Greece they preferred to remain with European union and accepted some extremely harsh terms and conditions to secure economic bailout package and money to repay its debt, now it would have made world of sense for the Greeks to break ties with European union and abandon Euro currency, which would have given them opportunity to reintroduce their very own currency **Drachma**, with Greece's own currency, and their own independent monetary and industrial policy, the Greeks then would have succeeded in rebuilding their country, developed their tourism industry and by devaluing their own currency Drachma Greece would potentially have become low cost manufacturing hub in Europe, so had Greece's politicians shown greater maturity and broken ties with European union, there would have been short term initial pain, but over medium to long term Greece citizens would have substantially benefited. Also independence to decide its own political policies would have helped Greece frame its own immigration policy and that would have helped Greece be in a better position to deal with refugee and migrant crisis.

Folks should keep in mind that "Commercial Banks are not humanitarian institutions" but they are lenders, so when a bank lends you money it is also their job to recover money back from you, therefore even while using your Credit Card to make payments at top tier restaurant or in upscale shopping mall, keep it in your mind that you'll also have to pay back money that you spend today, so be within your limits, your reckless spending will make coming generations bankrupt. Lending money is risky business. Even when the borrower pledges a collateral that the lender can confiscate and sell to recover the lent funds, shifts in economic fundamentals can render the loan worthless. The term toxic debt has been used loosely and encompasses a wide variety of loans, but usually refers to mortgages and mortgage-backed loans that became nearly worthless in the first decade of the 21st century.

Article title "**Toxic Loans Around the World Weigh on Global Growth**" explains; "Beneath the surface of the global financial system lurks a multitrillion-dollar problem that could sap the strength of large economies for years to come. The problem is the giant, stagnant pool of loans that companies and people around the world are struggling to pay back. Bad debts have been a drag on economic activity ever since the financial crisis of 2008, but in recent times, the threat posed by an overhang of bad loans appears to be rising. China is the biggest source of worry. Some analysts estimate that China's troubled credit could exceed $5 trillion, a staggering number that is equivalent to half the size of the country's annual economic output.

Official figures show that Chinese banks pulled back on their lending in December-2015. If such trends persist, China's economy, the second-largest in the world behind the United States', may then slow even more than it has, further harming the many countries that have for years relied on China for their growth.

But it's not just China. Wherever governments and central banks unleashed aggressive stimulus policies in recent years, a toxic debt hangover has followed. In the United States, it took many months for mortgage defaults to fall after the most recent housing bust — and energy companies are struggling to pay off the cheap money that they borrowed to pile into the shale (shale oil) boom.

In Europe, analysts say bad loans total more than $1 trillion. Many large European banks are still burdened with defaulted loans, complicating policy makers' efforts to revive the Continent's economy. Italy, for instance, announced a plan last week (of January-2016) to clean out bad loans from its plodding banking industry.

Elsewhere, bad loans are on the rise at Brazil's biggest banks, as the country grapples with the effects of an enormous credit binge."..........

One Fat medical bill or one failed crop (agriculture crop) can severely impact the living standard and lowers social status of the affected family, reduces status from upper middleclass to lower middleclass.

Yes, it is true that medical science and technology have made remarkable progress, our intelligent Scientists and Engineers have developed advanced scientific technology, all kinds of brutal ailments and diseases can be treated and be cured, but very few people in the world can afford or have access to best medical-care facilities and medical treatments, otherwise, for the large population of the world when they experience any kind of serious health problems like for example "fatal injuries, cancer, diabetes or cardio problems," for an average person around the world it is so difficult to have or to afford best quality medical treatment because it is so damn expensive, according to some estimates it has been found that staggering 75% of the world's population is medically vulnerable and can't afford to pay steep medical bills it is beyond their reach and means.

Citizens of rich developed countries do enjoy some privileges, government healthcare and services departments of developed countries do provide best possible basic medical healthcare facilities to their citizens, also medi-care insurance policy is available to be purchased at affordable price, but for the rest of the countries in the world and large population living in developing and 3rd world countries things are extremely difficult, people living in poor undeveloped nations for example Indian sub-continent countries and in African countries large percentage of population are so desperately poor that they can't even afford to buy simple basic medicines like Cough syrup, nose drops, or eye drops.

Affordability or unaffordability is one of the factor, whether or not if a person living in an underdeveloped country can afford to buy medicines and afford best possible medical treatment, as it is said that "health is wealth," what we need in the country where we live in must have efficient and well organized medical system and well entrenched healthcare facilities, but there apparently in another bigger perspective, for inadequate and appalling healthcare facilities and service in many of the underdeveloped and 3rd world countries, and that is because of widespread corruption and mismanagement of public healthcare system.

Most of the medical practitioners and medical staff and professionals in developing and 3rd world countries or for that matter perhaps even in developed countries have inadequate, insufficient and incomprehensible knowledge about medical terminology, medical diagnosis of patient and understanding of medicines, and most of the medical professionals and doctors often goof up majorly in diagnosing their patients and often make erroneous assumption and renders inappropriate medical treatment and prescribes incorrect medicines. Here have a listen to this, there is a joke on the street in Indian cities that "India's Medical and Public healthcare system is more corrupt than compare to India's political system," yes, Indian sub-continent countries which also includes countries like Pakistan and Bangladesh there is high level of corruption in medical and healthcare system, the healthcare facilities and medical services in Indian sub-continent countries is thoroughly disorganised and inefficient. Do some reality check and you'll discover the true reason as to why in so many countries the Public healthcare facilities are so appalling, and the most likely reason is that in India, Pakistan or in African countries like Nigeria and in several south-American countries large percentage of practicing doctors and other medical professionals have allegedly obtained medical degrees and certificates by fraudulent means.

In India for example it is allege that a person who wish to become "Doctor, lawyer or engineer" and if he/she is able to or willing to spend 2 or 3 million Rupees, so a person who is willing to spend money can conveniently obtain higher educational and diploma certificates and degrees, so be it India, Pakistan, China or Nigeria the education system itself is devastatingly corrupt, any person who has money and influence can easily manipulate the system and can win favours for himself/herself and obtain top tier jobs.

The economic costs of epidemics are often out of proportion to their death toll. The outbreak of Severe Acute Respiratory Syndrome (SARS) in 2003 is estimated to have caused over $50 billion-worth of damage to the global economy, despite infecting only about 8,000 people and causing fewer than 800 deaths. That is because panic and confusion can be as disruptive as the disease itself. Studies of past outbreaks have shown that lethal diseases that lack a cure tend to provoke overreactions. This is true even if the risk of transmission is low, as is the case with Ebola.

In a widespread public healthcare emergency, there will be more people who need healthcare than there are resources available to help them. Making decisions about how to use these limited resources will be difficult. Hospital personnel and public health officials need to know how to make decisions in these difficult moments in a way that reflects the values of the communities in which those decisions will be made. Human history is undoubtedly stained with the blood of men, women and children killed in war, but it is disease that is the world's biggest killer - and it does not discriminate between race, creed or colour.

Governments walk a fine line between limiting the spread of a disease and causing needless disruption. Panic is avoided not just by combating an epidemic, but by being seen to do so. Transparency is important. By disclosing the extent of an outbreak, governments limit the spread of rumours and encourage an appropriate response from business and the public. But there is also the risk that weak governments will simply expose their impotence.

If healthcare is a problem, there are many other challenges to deal with in 21st century, one of the most pressing problem is hunger and poverty, according to some surveys and research studies have found Worldwide there are 1.5 billion people who can't afford to eat healthy nutritional food because they have little or no money, but there also is another reason behind hunger and starvation, that is brazen wastage of food, roughly one third of food produce in the world for human consummation each year --- approximately 1.3 billion tonnes – gets lost or wasted.

A report prepared by **"United Nation Environment Programme' Food Waste: The Facts**," has written; "When we scrape off our dishes after a large meal, too full to finish the remaining scraps on our plate, we rarely pause and think about the significance of our action. It seems routine to us: if we have leftover food scraps that are unfit for eating, shouldn't they be thrown in the garbage? Our routine practices, unfortunately, make it difficult for us to conceptualize the magnitude of global food waste. The problem is bigger than we think.

According to a recent report by UNEP and the World Resources Institute (WRI), about one-third of all food produced worldwide, worth around US$1 trillion, gets lost or wasted in food production and consumption systems. When this figure is converted to calories, this means that about 1 in 4 calories intended for consumption is never actually eaten. In a world full of hunger, volatile food prices, and social unrest, these statistics are more than just shocking: they are environmentally, morally and economically outrageous.
Let's start with some basic statistics about food waste in North America and around the world.

Worldwide Food Waste Facts
- Every year, consumers in industrialized countries waste almost as much food as the entire net food production of sub-Saharan Africa (222 million vs. 230 million tons)

- The amount of food lost and wasted every year is equal to more than half of the world's annual cereals crops (2.3 billion tons in 2009/10)

North American Food Waste Facts
- In the USA, organic waste is the second highest component of landfills, which are the largest source of methane emissions
- In the USA, 30-40% of the food supply is wasted, equalling more than 20 pounds of food per person per month."………………

Indeed money is the most significant and prominent requirement of every human, we need money every step of the way in our life, for Food, clothes, housing and education, we people simply can't survive without money, but yet there are billions who are surviving with very little money in their hands to spend.

Staggering 60% of global population falls under lower income category, India and China are the two most populous nations in the world, therefore not surprising maximum number of poor as well live in these two countries, India perhaps is the worst affected of the two, when it comes to measuring income and purchasing power, astounding figures according to estimates 380 million Indians are **acutely poor**, and in China nearly 400 million Chinese are categorised as low earning or lower income families or individuals.

What are those uncanny reasons for such high level of poverty in our world? There are wide variety and combination of factors and reasons for staggeringly high level of poverty in our world, some of the key reasons for increased poverty in world are, mismanagement of resources, terrorism, protracted and sustain wars, insurgency and civil wars in many countries around the world, corruption in high places, frequent natural disasters and also demographic problems. Such examples and reasons of poverty and inequality are no doubt real. But there are other deeper and more profound reasons for chronic global poverty which apparently are not discussed.

Brutal wars and violence, criminal activities and gun violence, also natural disasters and freak road accidents, railways and industrial accidents claims millions of lives annually, across the globe millions of people die unnatural and untimely deaths, and what is even more disheartening fact is, that, majority of people who die in violence or accidents are mostly young people below the age of 40, and even bigger worrisome reality is that many of these folks who die are the sole bread winner of their family, the world is losing young talented demographic, if so many young men and women lose their lives prematurely, and many among these young men and women are principle earning member of their respective families, so when they die or are seriously injured and wounded it leaves their family without any viable source of income, this in turn creates more fundamental social and economic problems.

Globally there is serious health-care and demographic problems, demographic challenges are far too many, different countries have different demographic problems, while rich industrialized nations like Germany and Japan have growing percentage of elderly population, also China because of its more than three decades long strict One child policy, however China did relax its one child policy beginning of year 2016, and has allowed parents an option of having a second child if they want to, however enough damage has already been done, China as well like many European countries have rising elderly population. While many wealthy and prosperous nations of world have large elderly population, it is the opposite in many underdeveloped and poor countries, in India for instance has significantly high younger demographic, according to some surveys as of 2014 60% of India's population is/was below the age of 35, similarly in Pakistan, Bangladesh and many other Islamic countries like Turkey and Egypt etc have huge younger population, so it is a major challenge and difficulty for the countries which have large younger population, such countries desperately struggles hard to serve interest of their respective country's large younger demographic, to provide good education and healthcare to youngsters is always a challenge for the government of any country, and even more difficult is to create new job and business opportunities for younger demographic.

Have rare insight and broader perspective for growing demographic problems particularly in developed western countries, falling fertility rates, many modern fashionable feminist White European women and also modern Black African women in 21ˢᵗ century have become more career oriented, preferring to focus more on developing professional career rather than to start their own family and become mother, so delaying marriage and differing pregnancy, postponing motherhood for considerably longer period of time, most White European or even Black African modern day women you'll see becomes mother for the first time only after they've celebrated their 30ᵗʰ birthday.

But in stark contrast to White European and Black African women, you'll see it that majority of Muslim girls and women at the time when they celebrate their 25ᵗʰ birthday they are already mother of 3 or 4 children, large population of Muslim community is socio-culturally conservative and do not adopt family planning methods, it is highly likely that average Muslim women even if she is working yet she will get married at early age and will not delay pregnancy, so it is not surprising that Muslim population percentage wise as compare to every other religious communities grows faster, birth rate within Muslims community is very high.

But there's another perspective as well with regards to global Muslim population, it is true that for past many years and decades Muslims are scoring higher points in terms of birth rate, but not many have observed another reality that the mortality rate or death rate among Muslims is high as well, it has been observe that Muslim women outlives Muslim men, life expectancy of Muslim women is higher than Muslim men, why? There are some ridiculously odd reasons as to why the death rate among Muslim is high, it is because in most of the Islamic rule countries in the world or Muslim dominated countries have nerve-wrecking history as well as ongoing reality of destructive wars and civil wars, besides have higher degree of terrorist attacks and communal violence, also some of the Islamic countries are prone to frequent natural disasters (earthquakes, tsunamis or floods) and extreme weather conditions (treacherous heat waves or extreme cold weather), so all these combination of reasons and factors are responsible for claiming many lives, considerably large number of Muslims particularly in Muslim dominated countries dies in wars and terrorists related or other form of brutal fights and violence. But despite so many Muslims dying unnatural death in violence and or due to harsh weather conditions, yet as of 2015 the world's Muslim population remains 1.6 billion strong.

The two most devastatingly dangerous problems and arguably the most difficult challenge before humanity is and if we humans fail to find quick solutions than it can potentially or rather most certainly will destroy entire humanity, and these two problems are **Terrorism and Weather (climatic problems)**, the most pressing concerns and biggest challenge before entire humanity in 21st century is wildly increasing religious intolerance, which apparently is giving rise to terrorism and causing social tension and communal disharmony, persistent incidents of brutal killings and violence has evidently ruin peace of mind of billions of people around the world, if self-radicalized individuals and fundamentalists forces whosoever is/are perpetrating crimes and terrorising Masses, frequent terrorist attacks is harming our society and those people who are responsible for killing thousands of innocent people each year around the world. Now, if most people firmly believe that terrorism is most dreadful evil and a menace that's harming and destroying humanity, No friends wait a moment don't blame terrorists alone, terrorism and religious fundamentalism is not foremost dangerous evil as it is thought or believed to be, because even bigger and most frightful and what is particularly causing immense pain to all we humans and which will eventually destroy all of us is the menace of Climate and Weather related problems, yes, imbalanced ecological systems, deteriorating earth's atmosphere, air pollution is damaging and impairing natural environment, so all the impairments and imbalances are causing frequent natural disasters in almost every part and corner of our **Planet Earth**, no region in the world is spared from menacing climatic weather related problems.

Some studies and surveys have discovered that Climatic weather related problems are unquestionably responsible for increase spread of diseases, and for rising poverty and hunger in our world, frequent natural disasters have displaced and have made millions of people homeless in many different countries around the world.

Who is responsible for promoting religious terrorism and for causing environmental problems? The answer, with regards to terrorism, it could perhaps be the selfish self-seeking politicians or the businessmen and perhaps also the religious hierarchy of prominent religions can be or could be blamed for aiding and encouraging terrorists activities and inciting violence. But for deteriorating Climatic conditions, one thing I can say with conviction that, it is without doubt the flawed and erroneous economic policies chiefly of the rich industrialized nations, which are explicitly responsible for damaging earth's atmosphere and causing environmental problems, **extreme Weather problems** like "Flash floods, typhoons, hurricanes, earthquakes, unseasonal rains," all such climatic problems are becoming all too common, frequent natural disasters are damaging properties, destroying agriculture farmland and causing unprecedented financial losses to governments as well to the common people.

If extremism and terrorism is bad enough evil and devastatingly harming humanity, deteriorating <u>natural environment</u> and <u>weather related climatic problems</u> is much more troublesome and much bigger menace, if we take into account the loss we humans have suffered due to frequent natural disasters, the loss of lives and financial losses that we humans have suffered is incredibly high, between 2001 and 2015 because of Warming oceans and changing climate has resulted in causing extreme weather patterns, all combination of factors are destroying world's ecological system and as a result of which frequent natural disasters keeps occurring across the world, millions of people have lost their life and have suffered trillions of U.S dollar worth of business loss and damages to properties and agriculture farmland.

The most notable among all natural disasters thus far in 21st century was the **high tsunami waves** that occurred in Indonesia and which also profoundly affected countries closer to it, primarily it was Indonesia that was most brutally affected that's because Indonesia was the first country to be affected by the massive earthquake in Indian ocean which caused high tsunami waves, the worst hit countries were Indonesia, Thailand, Sri Lanka and India, it happened on 26-12-2004 and over 230,000 people are reported to have died.

Indonesia and Philippine perhaps are most prone to natural disaster, but, even rich and developed countries as well are not spared, in fact the developed countries are experiencing some of the most horrific and extremely rough climate, increasing occurrence of severe weather, extreme weather events are a consequence of climate change and are becoming more frequent powerful and erratic, countries such as China, U.S, Britain, west-European countries and of course Japan, all these rich industrialized countries have suffered extremely high loss of business and properties and massive loss of lives of their citizens. Every continent has been affected, from one of the world's strongest storms hitting the Philippines and the widest tornado ever seen in the United States, to extreme droughts gripping central Africa, Brazil and Australia and a series of massive floods in Pakistan.

It is the rich industrialized nations who are in first place responsible for creating or causing irreparable damage to the **world's atmosphere**, it is their flawed and faulty economic policies that has or is destroying Planet earth's natural environment and ecological system and have put at risk lives of entire global population.

Not as much the terrorism but it is the climatic weather related problems which apparently is principle reason for economic uncertainty and ever rising hunger and poverty in the world. So, be it terrorism or climatic problems, both these crisis are man created, humans own created problems which are easy to solve yet no one wants to solve it, yes, it is we humans ourselves are incontrovertibly responsible for all our woes.

Between 2002 and 2015 natural disasters have destroyed livelihood of millions across the globe, ruining millions of acers of farm fields damaging standing crops, spreading dreadful diseases, rendering millions of families and people homeless.

What has caused more pain and extreme losses to humanity between terrorism and natural disasters? I don't have any data providing precise and accurate figures to quote but it is an obvious fact and safe for us to assume that less number of casualties and homelessness due to terrorism, but lot more due to frequent natural disasters across the world between 2001 and 2015 hundreds of millions of people have got displaced and become homeless besides losing their livelihood, apart from that > hundreds of thousands of people have lost their lives.

Now many among us believe and there is a general popular perception that if **Central Banks** keeps aiding industries and businesses by printing cash-currency notes it will help power economic growth and create massive demand for durables and consumer products, but do a reality check and you'll find that economic stimulus packages only creates bubble and in long term severely harms the economic growth and creates bigger social and political problems, thus far (as of 2015) in 21st century the world has witness two Boom and Bust cycle in Commodity markets, first between 2006/7 when prices of commodities hit record high levels particularly the price of crude oil which at one point traded at historic high levels of U.S$145 per barrel, and later in 2008/9 oil prices dropped below $40 per barrel, not only petroleum oil prices but prices every other industrial commodities fell and fell sharply lower as there was total carnage in commodity markets across the world as a consequence of 2008 global financial crisis, all base metals prices declined or rather collapse due to 2008 financial meltdown, banking financial troubles of 2008/9 plunged the global economy into deep recession, the financial crisis played significant role in failure of key businesses and declines in consumer wealth was estimated in trillions of U.S dollars, The active phase of the crisis, which manifested as a **liquidity crisis**, can be dated from August 9, 2007, when **BNP Paribas** terminated withdrawals from three hedge funds citing "a complete evaporation of liquidity. Sometime towards the end of 2008 the U.S Central Bank "Federal Reserve" taking bold initiatives but also perhaps most "convenient one" to halt deteriorating health of world's economy and U.S's in particular announced economic stimulus package QE (quantitative easing) and started printing fresh money in trillions of dollars, in subsequent months and years other countries as well started announcing their own QE programmes Japan, China and European central bank they all did what U.S did that was printing cash money, massive cash liquidity injected into the banking system and ultra-cheap credit made available to the businesses to borrow helped in reviving economic growth and trend reversal was led by stupendous China economic growth, due to heavy demand for industrial commodities and minerals and petroleum oil and gas from India and China the commodity markets started to recover back again in 2010, between 2011/13 the prices of almost all commodities rallied remarkably, Base-metals, precious metals, and more importantly the prices of petroleum crude oil & gas moved sharply higher.

The sharp increase in prices of various commodities between 2011 and 2013, tempted and encouraged the mineral mining companies to extract more minerals from beneath the surface of earth, and oil exploration companies drilled more oil wells to pump out more oil and gas, the manufacturing industries in China kept producing more industrial goods and consumer products, but what goes up has to come down, China's economic growth considerably slowed down beginning of 2014, due to demand recession for consumer products, and over production and excessive supply of minerals and petroleum oil and gas, created glut in the international markets, incredibly high production of durables and consumer products on assumption that demand for consumer items will only keep growing, but contrary to high expectation there was a subsequent sharp decline in demand for durable goods which caused a monumental fall in prices of commodities in 2015, massive drop in China's stock-markets in June –July of year 2015, demand for luxury items and for other consumer product further declined because the Chinese purchasing power reduced considerably, sharp fall in commodity prices that began in middle of 2014 and continued to fall and remained at lower level throughout year 2015 literally ruined the economies of resource dependant countries, turbulent in commodity markets caused uncertainty in Forex currency markets, Russia, Venezuela, Saudi Arabia, Iraq and Brazil etc all such major commodity producing and exporting countries suffered immense pain and economic hardship, due to decline in prices of commodities they produce and sharp fall in value of their respective country's currency, substantially reduced and eroded the purchasing power of resource dependant countries governments and of their citizens, when domestic economy is greatly affected by commodity price shifts, then that country's currency exchange rate is especially vulnerable, but not just commodity producing nations suffered economic troubles, also other countries as well suffered extreme hardship and uncertainty in forex and commodity markets considerably slowed down their economic growth.

Digging tunnels into the earth's crust, to extract minerals buried underground, digging and drilling deeper and deeper holes to extract minerals from the ground, to make and earn more money quickly and easily without any concern or remorse as to how much excessive mining and exploration will or could harm environment and cause climatic problems. Due to QE (quantitative easing) and frequent economic stimulus packages of rich industrialized countries in the aftermath of 2008/9 financial crisis to spur global economic growth, easy cash liquidity made available in the banking system had enticed and encouraged companies in the business of mining and oil & gas exploration to produce more output, due to massive increase in production of crude oil and other minerals like Iron-ore, copper and bauxite etc," supply exceeds demand, so slowing global economic growth which apparently reduced demand for various industrial commodities, hence due to huge oversupply of various commodities and large pile up of unsold inventories mainly of finish durable goods, so combination of factors like large pile of input materials both raw materials as well as of finish items and products in some of the prominent industrialized nations, so reduced demand caused monumental decline in prices of commodities in international commodity markets in 2015.

Uncertain situation became even more uncertain, the beginning of year 2016 proved to be nightmarish not only for the commodity producing and exporting countries but for the entire world's financial markets, in January-2016 prices of petroleum crude oil suffered bigger loses when prices declined below U.S$30 per barrel, Investors were jittery because of uncertainty in commodity markets which apparently created problems in Forex markets besides uncertainty with regards to future of principle resource dependant and commodity producing countries, nervous investors started unloading their investments apart from mining and oil exploration companies banking and financial companies share values fell sharply on major bourses across the globe.

Mounting concerns and worries about rising fiscal budget deficits of large commodity producing and exporting countries, hence assessing the ground realities for the first time ever perhaps in Jan-2016 trade analysts and economists started predicting that two of world's biggest oil and gas producing countries **Saudi Arabia** and **Russia,** there were/are apprehension amongst economists that if crude oil and gas prices remains subdued and keeps trading in lower range for longer period of time than these two prominent oil producing and exporting countries will be financially bankrupt, not just the Saudis and Russians but many other principle commodity producing countries would suffer extreme economic and social pain if corrective steps not taken and quick solutions not found. When there is a problem obviously we need to find a solution, now with regards to these beleaguered resource dependent nations economic problems which needs amicable solution, so now, if to fix economic problems if same measures is used that is of Printing money, create more cash liquidity to create bigger demand for consumer products, well I'm afraid printing more money to create more demand for durables and consumer goods may perhaps give a short term respite, but over longer term will only harm humanity and increase global warming and cause more climatic problems.

Monumental decline in commodity prices in 2015/16 had nasty economic and social consequences and had devastating negative impact on global economic growth and destroyed livelihoods of millions of people, Hundreds of billions of U.S Dollars that were earlier earmarked for massive expansion and or for new business investments in mining minerals and oil and gas exploration projects had to be either suspended for indefinite period of time or cancelled all together, also many existing companies in business of oil & gas exploration and mineral mining because of sustain lower profitability and losses suffered had to adopt drastic measures and were compelled to reduce workforce, hundreds of thousands of people lost their jobs, the magnitude and negative effects of **Commodity Crisis** in 2014/15 which precipitated problems in Forex (foreign exchange currency) and Capital markets were more severe and brutal than compare to 2008/9 financial crisis.

An asset bubble can be also aggravated by a supply shortage, if investors think there isn't enough of the stuff to go around. Asset bubbles are often initially caused by **low interest rates**. Low rates create an over-expansion of the >**money supply**. Investors can borrow cheaply, but can't receive much return on bonds, so they look for another **asset class**. A speculative bubble is usually caused by exaggerated expectations of future growth, price appreciation, or other events that could cause an increase in asset values. This drives trading volumes higher, and as more investors **rally** around the heightened expectation, buyers outnumber sellers, pushing prices beyond what an objective analysis of intrinsic value would suggest. Prices rise quickly over a short period of time, and are not supported by underlying demand for the product itself. It's a bubble when investors bid up the price beyond any real sustainable value. This price spikes often occur when investors all flock to a particular asset class, such as the stock market, real estate or commodities. The bubble is not completed until prices fall back down to normalized levels; this usually involves a period of steep decline in price during which most investors panic and sell out of their investments.

Economic bubble in **Japan** from 1986 to 1991 in which **real estate** and **stock market** prices were greatly inflated. The bubble was characterized by rapid acceleration of asset prices and overheated economic activity, as well as an uncontrolled money supply and credit expansion. More specifically, over-confidence and speculation regarding asset and stock prices had been closely associated with excessive plummeted to half its peak by the time of the fifth monetary tightening by the **Bank of Japan.** By late 1991, the asset price began to fall. This decline resulted in a huge accumulation of **non-performing assets loans** (NPL), causing difficulties for many financial institutions. The bursting of the Japanese asset price bubble contributed to what many call the **Lost Decade**.

There is no doubt that a global climate regime on the basis of international cooperation is needed to prevent some of the disastrous consequences of climate change. Its challenge is that it must include the commitment of developed countries such as the U.S. and the EU (European Union) as well as the commitment of large developing countries that have fast growing economies and a rapid increase in emissions such as China and India. This is difficult because it raises questions of global climate justice, historic liability and equal rights, i.e. whether developing countries should enjoy the same right to economic growth based on fossil fuels as the industrialized countries have experienced over the past century. Even if environmental costs were distributed equally to every person on earth, developing countries would still bear 80% of the burden (because they account for 80% of world population). As it is, they bear an even greater share, though their citizens' carbon footprints are much smaller. To solve critical Economic and social problems one needs to apply their mind, you need to have high quality **analytical skills** and more importantly need to have **critical thinking skills** so that your mind can think of creative ideas to solve critical and complex problems.

That's exactly what is not happening, the Central banks governors, the economic advisors and policies planners, the thinkers and decision makers and decision takers around the world it seems have seriously ran out of ideas. To ensure sustain economic growth and to improve standard of living of citizens of your country, the government officials, bureaucrats and politicians need to step out of their staggeringly decorated offices and needs to work on ground level, it is only through hard work that we can get sustain and equal economic growth and business development, such **short-cut measures** when politicians and government officials think that we'll keep printing unlimited amount of money as long as it is needed and everything will take care of itself and every other things will automatically get sorted out, in 21st the economists and policy planners of leading industrialized countries and Multilateral Development Banks feels that no need for us to step out of our office, just order Printing more money and all will be fine.

No dear, **Quantitative Easing** only help fuels rally and boom in stock-markets and property markets and share value of few prominent companies rises higher and higher thereby helps increase wealth and net-worth of few influential people, rich becomes richer and a person who is millionaire becomes billionaire, and that's why each time stock-markets fall 8 or 10%, one of the leading industrialized country high ranking central bank officer will come forward and assures the market players that their central bank is ready to do more, which obviously means ready to print more currency notes, frequent economic stimulus packages only helps few voracious and egocentric individuals and affluent families make oodles of money, for the rest of the world's population it is only hard work provided they manage to find job for themselves or else its only misery.

In the 14th century, **Moroccan** traveler and scholar **Ibn Battuta** made a long journey to Africa and Asia. He reached China in April 1345 after a stay in India before serving as an envoy of **Sultan Muhammad Tughlaq** of the Indian **Tughlaq dynasty** to China. He wrote "China is the safest, best regulated of countries for a traveler. A man may go by himself on a nine-month journey, carrying with him a large sum of money, without any fear. Silk is used for clothing even by poor monks and beggars. Its porcelains are the finest of all makes of pottery and its hens are bigger than geese in our country.".

While rest of the world enviably looks at China's economic growth prospect, and large Multinational companies and bankers are keen to invest their money in china hoping to earn higher returns on invested capital, but it seems the China's nationals at least some of the Chinese are it seems less optimistic about China's long term economic growth prospect or may be some wealthy Chinese feels less secure to have their money invested in domestic Chinese companies, business and properties or their money deposited in China's commercial banks, that seems to be the most likely reason because between 2010 and 2015 thousands of super rich and wealthy

Chinese have taken their money out of China and it has been reported that they've invested substantial amount of money overseas, money earned by fair means or allegedly by unfair and corrupt means, most conservative estimates suggest that the rich Chinese have invested well over U.S.$200 Billion buying assets and properties in countries like Australia, U.S.A, U.K and few other prominent countries, walk on the streets of any American or Australian cities and you will see many Chinese owned businesses, properties and homes.

When declining trend first began to emerge and there were imminent signs of slowdown in China's manufacturing sector in the beginning of 2013, to prevent downslide the government authorities and China's Central bank did what other developed countries Central bankers do, they as well started lowering interest rates and injected massive amount of fresh Cash liquidity into their banking system for obvious purpose that was for common people and for the businesses and industries to borrow more money, when returns on fixed income debt paper and bank deposits are low and unattractive, especially the middle-income and lower middle income individual people and families finds another alternate investments avenue and where else will they invest their money but in stock markets, it is alleged that the Chinese government authorities had subtly encouraged the lower middle income Chinese folks to invest their money in China's stock markets, when large number of people started investing money in China's stock markets there was a spectacular spurt in 2014/15 witnessed in the China stock-markets, valuations of listed Chinese companies extraordinarily kept rising, but then came the inevitable crash, in June and July of 2015 China's stock market fell nearly 50% from its peak, as it always happens many of those unfortunate lower middle income folks lost their money and lost it heavily, so the steep losses that millions of Chinese suffered due to stock market crash it caused further harm to China's economic growth. What is or what was required to do initially when there were visible sign of imminent economic slowdown, it was for the China's Central bank "**People's Bank of China**" to have aggressively **devalued** its currency **Yuan** against other major international currencies, China's Central Bank by strongly devaluing its currency would have also succeeded in restricting the outflow of money from China, a move that would have prevented rich and alleged corrupt Chinese from taking money out of their country, and also would have added much needed strength to its tiring manufacturing sector and perhaps would have saved many job losses.

There is this misconception in minds of many or to say it is a myth that lower commodity prices benefits companies and helps spur economic growth of principle commodity importing countries, now like China's economy registered considerable slowdown in 2014/15, similarly China's neighboring country India's economic growth has also been tepid or even worse than that of China. This is a false perception created by many that massive fall in commodity prices significantly helps growth of commodity importing countries, India is principle importer of many commodities, particularly India imports substantial quantity of petroleum crude oil and gas, despite 65% fall or slide in prices of crude oil, yet India's economy between July-2014 and December-2015 has remained lukewarm, but Indian government agencies according to some vague mathematical calculation published figures which quoted 7% plus annual economic growth, however we need to do some real reality check to discover the fact of as to how India's economy has performed during the period between July-2014 and December-2015, since July-2014 when internationally commodity prices started to decline and remained at lower level for the whole of calendar year 2015, during this period as per available information, Indian companies financial performance remained stubbornly below par, overall Indian corporates reported poor sales growth and profitability (bottom line) of most Indian companies remained weak, India's export fell between 24 to 28%, Indian Rupee in value fell against major international currencies, Indian Rupee against U.S Dollar fell 12%, India is world's 2nd most populous nation, hence it requires to create millions of job each year, but during this period as per figures published by government agencies only 525,000 new jobs were created not to ignore the fact that many businesses were shut during this period hence there were potential job losses, so there was appalling job growth rate in India, but more severe pain for Indian citizen was/is the exponential increase in prices of Food, prices of fruits, vegetables and medicines became unfordable for average Indian citizen and not to forget the fact that India has highest number of people living in poverty in the world. Adding more problems to Indian economy was sharp increase in Banks "Non-Performing asset loans (Bad loans/Debt)," more pain in form of rising unemployment and growing poverty, as 60% of India's population lives in rural India in villages hence rural population is overwhelmingly dependent on agriculture, and agriculture sector in India is worst hit, agro industry and farmers are considered backbone of India's economy but between 2014/15 thousands of debt-ridden and poverty stricken **farmers** in despair and agony committed suicides. So brutal fall of Chinese stock markets both Chinese and Indians trimming their expenditure because of subdued economic performance of China and India, this facts loudly and clearly indicates us that steep decline in commodity prices only exacerbate situation and further weakens economic fundamentals and does not augur to well at ground level.

With regards to India's great economic growth story, there was lot of hype and hoopla, between 2014/15, so much hype created in media, as if India has become economic superpower of the world, it was all creation of Rightist control media, even the western media fell prey, the western media without doing any ground work and never really bothered to have a ground level perspective and to do thorough reality check of ground reality in India to verify the facts, the western media as well over reported, overstated and over hyped India's economic growth story. India has as of 2015 population of over 1.25 Billion people, maybe few tens of million people in India are affluent and financially secured and have great spending power, but for remaining hundreds of millions of Indian citizens for them their day to day life is extremely difficult and distressful and devastatingly challenging to say the least.

The job of the government in each country has to be that of an regulator and monitor, and not of or be seen as manipulator, Capital & Financial Markets needs to be well regulated and the functioning should be transparent, administration and management needs to be made accountable, as long as market players are following the rules, government officers and ministers should not be concern and not lose their sleep over whether the listed companies share value (prices) are falling sharply lower or rising higher.

To understand more; touching base with another perspective "**Bad news is not Bad; yes, in fact, Bad news is considered Good news,**" it so happens that be it the U.S.A, Germany, China, Japan or any other or many more countries which have *Capitalist economic system*, whenever their respective country's **economic ministry or economic statistic department** publishes dismal economic data suggesting weaker economic growth, figures indicating lower GDP growth rate, rise in unemployment, drop in monthly retail sales, so whenever such dismal economic data are made public, a significantly prominent section of society, the Stock-markets traders and investors rejoice that moment and expectation runs high because investing community firmly believes that weaker economic growth will compel and force country's politicians and central bank to act decisively by taking more bold steps and measures to stimulate their country's economic growth, and obviously for that purpose the central bank chief will have to announce more liberal market friendly **monetary and credit policy**, and will inject higher amount of cash-liquidity into the financial system to stimulate economic growth, boosting public spending to increase consumption. The monetary and credit policies are well coordinated among central bankers of leading industrialized countries.

If printing money is not enough than as another measures to create cash liquidity in the system is to adopt **negative interest rate policy**, wherein the depositors do not earn interest for depositing money instead they have to pay charges or to say penalty to park their surplus cash with central banks or maybe even with regular commercial banks. As of 2016 few exemplary examples are **Bank of Japan** and **European Central Bank** are among few of those leading industrialized nations central banks which have adopted negative interest rate policy.

Central banks use their deposit to influence how banks handle their reserves. In the case of negative rates, central banks want to dissuade lenders (commercial banks) from parking cash with them. The hope is that they will use that money to lend to individuals and businesses, which in turn will spend the money and boost the economy and contribute to inflation.

It is also aiming to force investors to shift money out of bank accounts and into higher-yielding assets.

Since central banks provide a **benchmark** for all borrowing costs, negative rates spread to a **range of fixed-income securities**. By the end of 2015, about *a third* of the debt issued by euro zone governments had negative yields. That means investors holding to maturity won't get all their money back. Banks have been **reluctant** to pass on negative rates for fear of losing customers.

A negative interest rate means the **central bank** and perhaps private banks will charge negative interest: instead of receiving money on deposits, depositors must pay regularly to keep their money with the bank. This is intended to incentivize banks to lend money more freely and businesses and individuals to invest, lend, and spend money rather than pay a fee to keep it safe.

"Don't keep the **Powder dry**;" central banks actually coercing commercial lending banks and financial institutions to lend money to industries and businesses and also to individual people without any rational thinking and without dwelling much about borrower's repayment capacity, also exerting psychological pressure on individual people that for higher returns invest their savings and money in high-yielding assets, but for higher returns on capital to invest money in stock-markets or in precious metals (gold, platinum etc), or in high-yielding junk bonds or if in property, such investments are not without risk but full of risk and higher degree of uncertainty.

Wealthy families and business lobbyists mounts pressure on politicians and politicians and bureaucrats in turn puts pressure on central bank chief to take pragmatic steps and announce market friendly Credit and Monetary policy, with sly motive to create asset inflation, to ensure boom in stock-markets, so the mantra is borrow more spend more, but does anyone bothers or is ever concern about that those businesses and individual people who'll borrow money also have to repay money.

When inexpensive loans and abundant cash credit is easily made available, when borrowing cost are lowered to record low levels, nature of people as well of business owners in general is to take advantage of prevailing situation, so when money is available easily and cheaply they get excited and tempted to borrow more and more money and frivolously overspend money on buying unwanted items. People in general and business owners in particular overindulging in speculating and gambling or starting non-sustainable and unproductive business ventures, over producing industrial goods and consumer products, and one day the inevitable happens when they have exceeded their spending limits and exhausted their purchasing power, they are unable to repay the money back to their creditors, that's the time when many lending institutions and Banks will have long list of large scale loan defaulters, and all these combination of reasons and factors and also when businesses fails obviously many people lose their jobs so than due to massive job losses it creates a brutal long lasting economic recession and which in turn causes too many social problems and troubles in society. Not only economic recession, but we also have to keep in mind that excessive mining of minerals and exploration of petroleum oil and gas, as minerals and crude oil is/are crucial raw material to manufacture all kinds and types of industrial and consumer products, so excessive mining to extract more minerals profoundly and severely harms environment and ruins earth's atmosphere, deteriorating weather condition is danger for each of us as it risk survival of humanity on this planet.

Humans are "eating away at our own life support systems" at a rate unseen in the past 10,000 years by degrading land and freshwater systems, emitting greenhouse gases and releasing vast amounts of agricultural chemicals into the environment, Most underground mining operations increase sedimentation in nearby rivers through their use of hydraulic pumps and suction dredges; blasting with hydraulic pumps removes ecologically valuable topsoil containing seed banks, making it difficult for vegetation to recover. Underground mining has the potential for tunnel collapses and land subsidence. It involves large-scale movements of waste rock and vegetation, similar to open pit mining. Additionally, like most traditional forms of mining, underground mining can release toxic compounds into the air and water. As water takes on harmful concentrations of minerals and heavy metals, it becomes a contaminant. Deforestation due to mining leads to the disintegration of biomes and contributes to the effects of erosion. Thus, a large-scale mining process can affect the environment, including the human environment miles away from the original mining site. Exposure to chemicals poisons the human body causing everything from skin rashes to cancer. Drinking water with lead and other chemicals can affect babies and cause birth defects.

In modern times most Central Banks adopting more liberal and easy **monetary policy** and easy Credit policy has have had brutal and killing impact on **Fixed income markets,** Fixed income which gives assured annual returns and considered highly safe, for hundreds of years in the past ages common people and investors used to invest their hard earn money and savings in Fixed income securities like Fixed deposit in Bank or Post-office, or they use to invest in government debt instruments and bonds, and use to earn decent assured annual income, in more recent times now in 21st century with banks having reduced interest rates to near Zero%, and government securities of many rich industrialized countries giving dismal 2% or 3% annual returns, even in many developing countries where interest-rate on bank fixed deposit or government bonds are in lower single digit, in times of distressfully lower banking interest-rates, many people are left with no other choice but to take risk of either investing their hard earn money in stock-markets or in "**triple B or C**" rated companies **junk bonds,** such investments which are high-risk and sometimes highly rewarding, and then there are also lunatics who invest their money in **Ponzi schemes** and end up losing their shirt.

I must say, that, 21st century politicians are ruthless because they are simply forcing humble people to take higher and higher unwise risk.

When so ever a country or the global economy is plunged into recession or when businesses are experiencing slowdown, so the best way and a good strategy of dealing with uncertain business environment is to allow the recession to run its course, as there is a saying "don't try catching a falling knife," don't try any desperate measures and take ill-timed decisions to contain recession, any massive fall or sharp downward price correction in stock-markets, should be welcomed because when share value of prominent companies are down and available at distinctly lower rates, it provides another large section of society an option or an opportunity to buy and to make investments in blue chip companies shares which are available at lower valuation. Therefore economic recession is not always a bad thing to happen, at times recession opens up windows of opportunities for large section of society and gives another chance or an opportunity for wide section of society to take calculated risk and to succeed in life by investing their time and money in promising business ventures.

Here I would like to emphatically and categorically like to say, that NOT the Islamic Terrorism or terrorists that we humans need to fear most, but, it is the Central Bank chiefs, those people responsible for printing unprecedented amount of cash money, to artificially spur their own country's as well to boost global economic growth, are actually the biggest enemy of humanity, it is they (central bankers) who will be responsible for destroying humanity and not the Islamic terrorists as many of you folks fear and wholeheartedly believe they will.

We need to think about life from many different perspective, we all know about the superlative strength that **Power of Money** have, we need to learn Artistic skills to earn money, perhaps it may be easy for many to earn money and lots of money and become super rich, but, Not many people realizes that it may perhaps be easy to earn money but it is even bigger and difficult challenge, as in, how to spend the money you've earned. What is measured also need to be managed, most people goof up big time because they become rich with considerable ease, but they don't know how to effectively use power of money as they haven't learn the skills of spending money, it requires skills to effectively and purposefully spend the money you have.

We listen to lots of stories of people rising from Rags to Riches, when a person obtains wealth and becomes a millionaire, such news stories are extensively written and discussed and hyped a lot, but there are more stories in history of people falling from **Riches to Rags**.

Those of you, who observe and keep track of things and events happening around, must be knowing the fact that some people become rich in much shorter period of time, but as sooner they become rich equally faster they become poor.

Some millionaires and billionaires comprehensively fails to preserve their wealth.

What is the difference or what is the meaning - in being Rich and in being Wealthy?

In all practicality it means the same, being Rich or Wealthy there is No difference.

However there is more subtle meaning and difference in being Rich or in being Wealthy.

Subtly if we do comparison to find out the difference between being "rich and wealthy," it is all about the way in which a person Thinks and his/her Behavioural habits.

A person who is Rich will be extravagant and a bit whimsical.

A wealthy person will be more circumspect and clever.

A rich person will like to dominate the scene and like to be in limelight all the time.

A wealthy person would like to maintain low profile and will make friendship with select few likeminded individuals.

It is the choices and decisions a person makes whether he/she have lots of money or lot less money.

When some people become super rich in short period of time or some by default becomes rich overnight, especially talking about the Rich and Famous, like the

Athletes and other sporting personalities like footballers and boxers, or Fashion models and movies stars, singers and dancers or those fortunate people who win lottery ticket, once they become lot richer and have lots of cash at their disposal, often they tend to make many wrong choices in terms of using and spending their money.

Few of the most common habits that most rich people have is, over spending their money on vacations, frequently eating out in top tier restaurants, staying in expensive hotels, regularly throwing lavish parties in grand style and frequently organising get to gather, purchasing unwanted luxuries items, reckless shopping buying stuff which they hardly use, over-eating food.

Ill-timed and ill-advised bad investment decisions, Bad business partner/partners, are some of the key reasons and potential causes in many peoples misfortune and loss of money, all these wide variety of factors means -- fall from Riches to Rags.

A person who is wealthy will meticulously plan investment strategy and will insure he/she makes timely move and make investment in low-risk business projects, buying properties or otherwise investing in any kind of financial instruments at appropriate time, also accordingly allocates funds for personal and business expenditure.

Rich folks are notorious spendthrift, a person who is rich always likes to do things in grand manner and fashion, like for example; eating out in upscale restaurants too often, always prefers to celebrate there's and their family members birthday, organising lavish birthday bashes, whenever there is an auspicious occasion like wedding of a family member they will like to spend big amount of money ensures there's is a big fat wedding and party will be organised in the best possible hotel in town. Rich folks will spend money giving expensive gifts to friends and relatives and will also give generous donations to charitable trust etc.

In some cases and instances it so happens, that, as a young children born in lower income household, when they walk down the street in their locality, they see posh restaurants and cafes serving exquisite cuisine, when these children feels tempted to eat food items like Cakes, ice-creams, pizzas they see and realizes that they don't have money in their pockets, they also see fancy clothes only from outside in the showcases of Clothes stores and fashion boutiques, as they can't afford to buy the items they crave to buy, but, when one day, when one among these children with great luck becomes Rich and becomes a Millionaire, that's when they start thinking now is the momentous moment in our life, they start feeling that they are now accomplished humans, and now is the time to fulfil all our dreams, this is where things could potentially go haywire for some of them, some people who rise from Rags to Riches, they are at times unable to cope with the pressure of being rich, and they are unable to take care of their new found wealth, it so often happens when a person becomes super Rich and Famous, such Rich and famous individuals either becomes very lenient and generous or become extremely arrogant and selfish.

Lots of money in the pocket of any person gives him/her extreme sense of satisfaction, but it could also become traumatising, in rich and wealthy families at times, the power of money also becomes utmost cause of internal bickering and distrust among family members, family members becomes wary of each other, enormous stress and pressures confounds confusion and misunderstandings which can cause domestic violence.

Wilful Waste Makes Woeful Want, Money saved is money earned.

We all perhaps may have heard this story; "The Goose that laid Golden Eggs," The Hen that Laid golden eggs, so, when a family have a Hen that is laying golden eggs, that family can go into relax mode, as the family have a Hen which everyday provides them a golden egg, which means easy source of resources, no need to work hard, with lots of cash in hands, it helps family live a fancy luxurious life, the family becomes complacent, but, does anyone ever advice the same family, that, what will happen to you all once the Hen that is laying golden eggs will be No more? Yes, what will happen to the family when the Hen that lays golden eggs either dies or for some apparent reason stops laying golden eggs?

When in life, the going is good and money is earned easily without much of an effort, people tend to become complacent, I would like to give a word of advice and would like to caution folks of imminent danger of becoming complacent and frittering your hard earn money, so, always think a step ahead, always think and care about your future, whether we talk about an individual families or businesses, corporates or the countries governments, **never rest on your laurels**. Time is precious, Time is mightier, Time is loaded with many possibilities and which of the possibilities will play out and when, time alone knows about it.

Have a listen to this, **"Life is pregnant with many possibilities, which of the possibilities will play out, how and when, time alone will tell**," beauty will dissipate in matter of moments, wealth will evaporate without any warning.

For example; I would like to tell a brief but very interesting story to provide better perspective and to understand how important it is to be careful with spending money, have a listen: "there is a young man who is 32 years old, and he has a family of two children and wife, one day this young man gets big promotion in his office where he works plus he gets massive hike in salary, a Six figure annual salary package "U.S $250 Thousand," the young man returns home jubilant, with big pay package, means increase disposable income, he feels confidence and embolden with more cash in his hands, he starts buying luxury items, upgrades his car and buys another extra car, refurnishes his house, to impress his guest he buys expensive Art Works and Paintings and adorns the walls of his home with artistic paintings, frequently goes out to eat in top tier restaurants, takes his family out for vacations to exotic locales, celebrates his children and his own birthday in style invites lots of friends and relatives, feeling confident about his job and his hierarchal position in his company, he also doesn't hesitate in borrowing personal loan from bank to meet his ever rising extravagant expenses, so this young man lives life king size, life goes on happily, 5 years have passed since this young man got promotion, everything is going well, now this man age is 37, one day the management of the company informs this young man that the company No longer needs his service and terminates his duty, now this young man who had high paying corporate job with staggering annual salary, has lost his job, and to his dismay there aren't any suitable jobs available for him, with no source of income, but this beleaguered man has run huge credit card debt and has taken big personal loan from bank, heavily debt ridden, plus he has to support his family, what will he do now?"…….. indiscipline and irresponsible behaviour is what precipitates mid-life crisis, and solutions are hard to find.

When going is good and conveniently things are happening in life, at that point in time people tend to become complacent and starts living life frivolously, they take things lightly.

Time and circumstances can change at any time without a notice. Don't devalue or hurt anyone in life. You may be Powerful today, But remember Time is more powerful than you.

The fun and satisfaction is always in increasing our wealth, when wealth is passed on to Gen-Next, which means, when older generation passes the wealth to younger generation, the responsibility on younger generation is to take their wealth to the next level, they need to strive to multiply the wealth they've inherited from their parents and grandparents, if siblings brother and sister inherits wealth from their parents then the responsibility increases on them to take wealth to next level of success by meticulously planning expenditures, making strategic well-timed investments which eventually gives higher cash returns hence earns them more money, as it is that we need money to earn money, so the siblings needs to enhance their wealth which their parents have graciously passed on to them, and Not to squander and fritter with the Millions of Dollar worth of assets, cash and properties they have got on unproductive expenses like "throwing splendid parties, long holidays at sumptuous locales, buying extraordinarily expensive designer fashionwear, writing big cheques and donating huge amount for extraordinary causes." Rich folks likes doing substantive things and in style to remain significantly relevant in society.

It is very important that we take life seriously and nurture our resources well, or else be ready to face unimaginable but inevitable consequences in life.

When wealthy individuals spends their money wisely and invest their money in high-yielding business projects or else by spotting talented individuals who has/have the appropriate skills and required talent, thus giving him/her much needed financial support to start a business venture, this is what creates more wealth for the wealthy and provides job opportunities which helps considerably in alleviating poverty, do something that brings prosperity to you and equally helps in lifting the living standards of the vulnerable section of society in more meaningful way.

Losing our money hurts us more than anything else, it is so important for us, not to take undue risk and lose our hard earned money, calculated and calibrated risk taking may often give us big rewards, but **Reckless Risk** almost always results in big loss and brings agony in our life, most people whether they are from lower middle class or rich affluent class likes too or gets tempted to dabble with their cash savings, some desperate folks even do not hesitate in borrowing cash to invest in speculative financial instruments to make quick bucks, placing speculative bets on sports (match-games) or on the outcome of election results are common practice also betting their money on horse racing is what most people enjoy doing, but most favourite and favoured place for those diehard risk takers is Stock-Markets, many people around the world gets lured and likes to either speculate or invest in Stock-Markets buying Shares of companies they think price movement of the scrip they are investing in will be favourable and to their liking hence enable quick monetary gains, each investor thinks he/she is a champion or the professionals whose advice they are seeking is/are champions and they cannot go wrong in their decision of investing or speculating, No dear, cloud movements can be predicted but Stock & Commodity Markets movements can never be easy it is always difficult to predict, if it was/were so easy to predict the "**Capital markets**" No one in this world would have been living in acute Poverty, the world would long have been freed of hunger and poverty.

Whether a junior bank employee or a taxi driver loses U.S $200 or a rich wealthy businessman loses U.S$20000 either investing or speculating in financial markets buying/selling shares of companies, whether a person loses $200 or $20000, it is money after all, it pains severely to the person who loses his/her money.

That's why, it is said, that, "**Money saved is Money earned**" at least save what you have of your own. Don't try short cuts.

Greater Fool theory, is an interesting topic, some may find it funny, some may find it humorous frankly even I think there is lot of humour, to understand what exactly is greater fool theory, when one fool finds a bigger and bigger finds even bigger fool than him/her; to put fools theory in perspective, have a listen to this, my own imaginative short story; "Once an Artist designs and creates a Painting, and goes to meet Art dealer at his Art gallery, he shows his work (Painting) to the owner of Art Gallery, the owner of the art gallery glances at the Painting and tells the Artist, good work done, we'll be able to Sell your painting for well over a Million U.S dollars, the Artist is ecstatic he hugs the owner of the Art gallery and queries with him, you think so, are you sure my painting can fetch me over a million dollar? The artist ask the Art gallery owner, but how? The owner of art gallery replies, by manipulation and manoeuvring, he elaborates further to explain the artist his plan, he says, I'll fix a deal with a renowned Art critic who will do evaluation of your work and he will give a favourable opinion about your Painting and certify it as a Classic Artistic work, he further says, once the art critic gives his favourable views than his views will be published in newspapers, once your painting is certified, we'll put your painting on the floor for Auctioning, the Artist is elated and emotionally charged, he expresses his gratitude to the owner of art gallery, the owner of art gallery gives an offer to the artist, he says I'll take 50% commission from whatever amount your painting sells for, the artist nods his head and agrees to the offer.

The owner of the art gallery contacts his friend who's an Art critic discusses and explains to him what he has to do, the art critic understands and commits to the owner of art gallery that he will give most favourable opinion and view about the said Painting, after the evaluation of painting is done and positive review gets published in newspapers, finally the Painting is put for Auction.

The Auction of the Painting is done and the Painting Sells for a massive amount, the buyer is an art lover who pays 2 Million U.S Dollars, the Artist who created and designed the Painting is exceedingly happy but also nervous and curious to know, why a buyer paid such a huge amount whereas it had cost the Artist only Two thousand U.S dollars to create the painting, the deal for his painting is done and payment is made and the buyer is ready to take the delivery of the Classic Painting and go, the Artist becomes impatient and out of curiosity walks up to the buyer of his painting and begins conversation by saying, Sir, thank you for buying my Painting, the buyer of the painting appreciates and tells the artist, you've done a fantastic job I liked your painting that's why I paid 2 million U.S.-dollars to buy your painting, the artist queries with the buyer of his Painting, don't you think you've paid a lot of money for my work, to be honest, my Painting is not worth the amount you've paid, are you? The artist stops himself from speaking any further, basically he wanted to tell the buyer of his painting are you crazy, but the buyer of the Painting understands what question/query the artist has in his mind and what actually he wants to know from him. The buyer ask the artist, did you meant to ask me am I a fool to pay such huge amount, the artist listening to his patron's comments feels embarrass but nods his head, softly says Yes, the buyer firmly replies, yes, I'm a fool to have paid 2 million U.S.-dollars to buy your Painting but you know, What? I'm a 1st fool, and There are even bigger fool than me, after few months I'm going to sell this painting and I'm drop dead sure it will sell for much higher price and I'll eventually make profit, after brief conversation with artist the buyer of the Painting takes delivery of painting and goes home.

After 6 months the 1st fool puts for sale the Painting he'd bought for 2 million U.S dollars, guess, what? He finds a bigger fool who buys the Painting and pays him 5 million U.S Dollars.

After another 6 months it's time for the 2nd fool to cash in on the deal and make profit from the painting he'd bought for 5 million U.S. dollars, the painting is put for sale and he finds a buyer, this is fool # 3, who pays astronomical sum for the painting, he buys the Painting for 10 million U.S dollars.

Few months later even the 3rd fool feels the urgency for selling the Painting which he has bought for 10 million U.S dollars, he goes to the art gallery and puts the Painting up for sale, wow, this fellow is lucky, he finds a buyer who is apparently fool #4, and he buys the Painting for whopping 15 million U.S Dollars.

Now after keeping the Painting in his home for nearly a year, the 4th fool as well thinks he must sale the Painting he owns for higher amount, he is convince that painting will sale for much higher price because by now there is lot of hype with regards to the Painting he has and owns, the Painting which apparently has become world famous, the 4th fool finally takes the Painting to the art gallery and puts it up for sale, now look at this, can anyone imagine, how lucky this fool# 4 is? He instantly finds a buyer for the most talked about Painting, the deal is struck for monumental amount "**20 Million U.S Dollars**" is paid.

(So the Painting which the original artist had prepared and it had cost him no more than just a paltry amount of Two Thousand dollars and which was first sold through an art gallery owner and dealer for 2 million U.S dollars, and couple of years later is sold for massive 20 million U.S. dollars).

The 5th fool after paying 20 million U.S dollars, takes home the painting with lots of fanfare, the 5th fool spends whopping 40 thousand dollars just to ensure safety and security of the Painting after all he has bought a Master's Art Classic Painting for 20 million U.S. dollars, the fifth fool organises a grand cocktail party at his home and invites his friends and business associates to have a glance at his 20 million dollar Painting.

One day misfortune strikes at the 5th fool house, due to adverse weather condition a brutal storm hits the house and damages big portion of the house and to his dismay the 20 million U.S dollar Painting is totally destroyed."..........

This is how life goes on; therefore, ensure you are not susceptible, do not get inspired by some false theories of inspiration, it is all in the mind of people, irrational beliefs, sometime people pay astronomical amount of money to buy rubbish, utter rubbish I must say, it's all sentiment driven and hyped, exaggerated and extravagant claims made particularly in advertisements and promotional material, hype drives people crazy, to say the least.

Life is about balance, Be kind, but don't let people abuse you, Trust, but don't be deceived, Be content, but never stop Improving yourself.

Globally, it seems there is a massive business overhaul and corporate restructuring plan underway, most of the new job opportunities that are being created are from the small businesses, after the collapse of leading investment banker "Lehman Brothers" in 2008 and subsequent financial meltdown due to the collapse of several of world's leading financial institutions which caused global economic recession, but thereafter the sluggish economic recovery has seen strongest growth in lower-end, low skill, Low-wage work, especially in Malls and fast food restaurants, the deep recession of 2008/9 primarily wiped out many high & medium salary paying jobs.

When employees and workers unions demands that minimum wages should be raised and fixed at higher levels, keeping in mind the rising cost of living and particularly keeping in mind the interest of lower-end employees who apparently finds it more difficult to cope with inflationary pressure, the employees resort to protest and strikes to exert pressure on their employers, the employers and management thinks the demand of their employees are unjust and initially opposes to give a pay hike but subsequently relents to what they (management) consider overbearing demands of their employees, hence, even though reluctantly but still the management does agrees to meet their employees demand and increases the minimum wages, but, even if the employees manages to win the battle of wits against their management and as per their demand gets minimum wage hike, but, **Corporate Profit** is what matters most to every management of each companies, therefore to neutralise the effects of pay hikes, the managers resorts to other means to avoid spending more money on their employees, in which case they (managements) either outsource their work to low cost country or they install Automated machines and Robots (Artificial intelligence) which helps the management to reduce the employees strength in their organization, so, when the employees wins the battle by getting at least minimum wage increased but they lose the war when crafty managements reduce the staff strength in their organizations. Which is becoming major reason for increase unemployment in most parts of the world.

What has also added to the woes in the job markets and proving a biggest obstacle in creating high paying jobs in industrial manufacturing sector and also in commercial sector is the sharp and comprehensive decline in prices of petroleum crude oil & gas and many other industrial commodities like copper, zinc, iron ore and coal etc, sharp decline in commodities prices which started in the middle of the year 2014 particularly monumental fall in crude oil prices, lower prices of commodities means lower profits or even loses for the companies in the business of commercial mining and oil & gas exploration, lower profits or businesses loses means No cash available with the companies, hence, No new investments in oil exploration and mining industries, worse still also the earlier planned new projects for commercial mining and exploration have either been abandon all together or put on hold, no expansion and diversification means No new jobs and business opportunities.

Revolutionary technology and innovation of new technology par excellence, trade experts and financial analysts are of the opinion that between 2015 and 2032 across the world over 100 million existing jobs will be loss and very few new jobs will be created, Artificial intelligence, robotic machines and automatic machines will replace humans at workplace and do most of the work.

Younger demographic facing financial challenges, but situation is far worse for middle-age people in their 40s and 50s, many of them experience mid-life crisis when they have no stable job and uncertainty over monthly income hence things become difficult, difficulty in paying monthly bills. People who feel that their financial outlook is unstable, economic insecurity causes physical pain and increases stress and anxiety.

Indeed traumatizing, experts from the field of medical science says, that worldwide 1 out of 3 person suffers from anxiety and depression, but due fear of social consequences, stigma and shame many people do not discuss their mental health problems with others, worse still they feel scare to discuss their mental illness even with their near and dear ones, therefore they hide it from their parents or children or siblings. "*Behind the smile of many is a hurting heart,*" have a close look and they are not what you see or they pretend to be, they are brutally broken from inside.

Because we humans are greedy that's what makes us more energetic, we crave for better living standards and for better tomorrow, and to make our life comfortable and to achieve our objectives and to fulfil our desire we think hard, our **Power of thoughts** helps us innovate technologies to suit our purposes, the first major breakthrough in human history which immensely helped in progress of us (humans) was some Twelve thousand years ago, when it is assumed the first Agricultural Revolution started, agricultural revolution dramatically changed the fortune of humans, agriculture revolution produced transformation of human society and brought unequivocal progress. Then the next big thing happened not until 18th century AD, here I'm referring to the beginning of first Industrial Revolution which apparently started in Britain sometime in the 1760s.

The foundation of great Industrial Revolution was first laid in Britain in 1760s, when for the first time humans shunned the primitive and medieval era technology and adopted new measures for which special- purpose machinery were designed and develop for mass manufacturing of products like "Textile and textile products and Iron and Steel," increasing use of Steam Power and Coal to generate electricity, helped Business transformation from handmade production methods to powerful machine manufactured products. In first phase of industrial revolution it was mostly textile and iron and steel products that were manufactured than the next big boost to industrial revolution was received in the form of Transport Revolution in 1870s onwards when Automobile technology was first researched than tested and later introduced, "Shipping, Railways, Roadways and biggest of all Aviation" surface, air and waters all mode of transport technology were upgraded between 1860s and 1910s, by 1920 Industrial Revolution had largely achieved its objectives. Industrial revolution initially started in Britain in 1760s but gradually spread to other parts of Europe and later across the ocean to U.S. and Japan and other parts of the world, U.S. is primarily credited with starting Transport revolution.

Then, the second phase of rapid economic growth and industrial progress started during and after the 2nd World War, between 1940s and 1980s, in this phase the manufacturing sector took a backseat and instead the Service Sector came into the forefront, Service sector businesses led by Banking, financial services, insurance, software and entertainment industry prominently registered sharp growth in business volumes.

Industrial revolution so vehemently improved the lifestyles and living standards of Billions of people around the world, millions of people became millionaires and moved into staggeringly beautiful abode, for rich or for the poor the life has indeed become a lot more easier now, then, it was in pre-industrial revolution era, in terms of comfort and for our convenience we have Electricity, telecommunication, lifesaving medicines, air-condition, fans, cooking gas, and so many other items of personal usage which all adds to the comfort of ours.

In any kind of economic revolutions be it industrial or agriculture, whenever new technology is invented and new products are introduced for the first time, the inventors who innovate and the engineers and scientists who work on the newly introduced innovated technology for them the biggest challenge and most difficult task always is to skill and reskill the existing labour workforce, as and when new technologies are invented either for service sector or manufacturing sector the skilled labour workforce is unavailable for obvious reasons, so for the innovators of technology it's a major challenge and uphill battle as they have to put in extra effort and work hard to teach and train to make potential technicians and users to understand the use and usage of modern technologies.

The best thing to have ever happen for we humans is the **Internet Revolution** also called the New Industrial Revolution, Commercial Internet service providers emerge for the first time in 1980s and by mid-1990s it had a revolutionary impact on society throughout the world, for majority of world's population Internet is/has become such an integral part of life that most of us feel our life is incomplete if we are not connected to the Net (internet), Internet technology has changed the dynamics of world's economy, with easy availability and easy access to information, the style and functioning of every businesses has changed because internet has opened doors of information like never before, internet technology has had profound impact on entire humanity, peoples habits, behaviour and lifestyles have seen dramatic changes, extensive use of internet service the world over helps people around the world to communicate with likeminded individuals and to socialize more freely.

Internet technology has provided platform for its users to maximise business productivity, it profoundly helps so many big and small businesses to realize true business success, to gain maximum benefits from internet technology, new age entrepreneurs for their start-up business can raise funds online, market their products and services and establish contacts with clients/customers all online. Social purpose for romancing and flirting or for commercial interest to cost effectively market and advertise our products and services, internet technology helps us all.

Once upon a time, it use to be everyone's dream to own and wear a German or Swiss made wristwatch, the Swiss and German wristwatches famous for its classic and opulence image, staggeringly gorgeous but frightfully expensive beyond the reach of many of us to afford it, but in more recent times in digital age, the perception has changed, in modern times you ask any young men on the street, whether you ask a young man on the street of "Mumbai or in Nairobi or Jakarta" put this question to him, asking him, What make and kind of wristwatch you like wearing? The answer most likely would be -- wearing a Apple smartwatch, Apple computers innovated smartwatch is what most of the young generation boys and girls, men and women prefer wearing most nowadays, wearable technology is most in demand in fast moving digitize world. Gold and silver jewellery and Swiss made wristwatches no longer finds much favour from consumers, the Fad is for Smartphones, smartwatches and smart eyewear's, Tablet computers, I-pad's and laptops. Sophisticated technological products are the preferred items on which consumers are willing to spend their money on.

In more simple term, consumerism is **Mind Game**, consumerism is social and economic order and ideology which encourages increasing consumption of goods and that's what is economically desirable, How to create consumer boom? What are the best brand promotion and marketing strategies? A lot depends on intrinsic value and quality of product/products and how good and strong is company's supply chain and distribution network, apart from more traditional commercial form of advertising methods, another method to popularize the branded product, which is **"Word of mouth advertising"** is most valuable and powerful form of marketing and popularizing consumer Products, When a person who buys product of a company and if he/she is satisfied and happy with the quality of the Branded product and finds it extremely useful and beneficial then the same customer will influence minds of many of his/her friends and acquaintance to use and buy the same product which he/she is using, so, our customers are our best brand ambassadors, you satisfy few of your customers with incredibly satisfying service and emphasize the fact to your customers, as in, how useful and beneficial it is for them to use your product than the same customers will help you win thousands more customers, so always value your customers aspirations because success of your consumer product to large extent depends on customers feedbacks, that is why "Word of Mouth" publicity is successful marketing and brand promotion formula, whether you are in business of selling smartphones or smartwatches or cheese cakes or fancy clothes word of mouth publicity is the best publicity, for increasing sales of your consumer product.

Fast evolving situation, brings about change in people's perception and conviction, new thinking, new ideas creates demand for new items and materials, that's good enough reason for businesses to keep in mind customers "needs, aspiration and requirements" and produce suitable products of consumers choice.

Innovation of new technology to develop new products and to refine existing services is most needed, the scientific research and development institutes works overtime to innovate and develop new technologies which is necessary to improve industrial productivity, to make businesses both manufacturing and service sector more efficient and effective, for enhance safety and security of humans, for clean and green environment purpose, new technologies always creates new jobs and provides new business opportunities, but the advent and introduction of new technologies also puts an abrupt end on future and career growth of many people as the existing technology which gets phased out once new technologies comes into effect, that means older staff of companies whether blue or white collar employees will need to reskill themselves and learn new business process technics if they want to become employable again provided there are job opportunities available for them.

When I was a child I use to listen stories from my mother about how in old times pigeons use to help humans, pigeons use to provide messenger service, were used as messengers, those were simple times. In older generations everything had to be handwritten, official correspondents and business account books everything had to be handwritten, not until 19th century sometime in 1860s for the first time a commercially successful and useable **Typewriter** was invented by **Christopher Sholes**, typewriters were great help for people around the world in fact still even in this modern era there are few people who still use typewriters, after invention of typewriters another significant technological breakthrough was Photocopy machines, then came electronic typewriters, even though computing technology was invented long ago but it was only in 1980s that computers became more visible to public, by the end of 20th century computers had become desperate necessity for people around the world, affluent class or underclass it is hard for most people to survive without computers and internet service in modern times, so this is what happened, since 1870s until 1980s typist, typewriters and typing was/were in great demand, millions of people around the world were either employed as typist or were working independently as typist offering service to people to type their letters and documents, but it all changed because change was need of the hour, as, since 1980s extensive use of new age technology and computers made typing and typist obsolete, after computers we've now got Ipads and Smartphones, we humans embrace technology for our convenient, we adopted computers because of preciseness and accuracy, computers helps us in more ways than one, it's not about emotions but about necessities, that we buy Hi-tech products for our betterment and to increase our productivity.

Things never always remains the same, in more recent times the Upgraded and modern Cloud Computing technology has/have changed the way Businesses operates and functions, let us understand, what Cloud Computing is and how it helps businesses? **Cloud Computing** is Conjugation of both Software and Hardware, in which software itself act as a hardware, Software fit on a chip can sell many value added computing programs-products-services offered through clouds is "Software as a service," Cloud computing is a green technology its environment friendly. Companies and even small business owners that uses Cloud Computing applications needs less staff, Cloud computing immensely saves time and money for businesses, companies incurs lower operational cost due to increase volume and higher productivity with fewer people, which means lot less manpower required because few employees can do lot more work. So, because of lower overheads and maintenance charges plus it further helps as it requires much smaller working space that's because less staff required hence fewer computers and other hardware devices are needed, all these combination of factors and inherent benefits adds up to increase productivity and higher profits for the companies.

These are the real life nightmares, extreme harsh reality of life, technological advancement and also periodic business overhaul severely undermines interest and career options of most people particularly that of degree and diploma holders, most highly qualified graduates and diploma holders remains unemployable or are underemployed because they have inadequate and inappropriate technical and clerical skills or lacks necessary talent.

Defeat teaches us many lessons, provided we are ready to learn from our past mistakes, victory at times makes person/persons complacent, hence, those unfortunates who have experienced defeat should try to recoup by keeping the disappointment of previous defeat at bay and needs to energise themselves, and with renewed optimism should vehemently move ahead in life to accept the next challenge, never run away from accepting challenges.

In fast evolving situation, in modern era, in 21st century when there is rapid change happening, technology advancing at faster pace, the product manufacturing procedures constantly keeps changing and processes are upgraded, like for example, Typewriter manufacturers had to abandon their production when Personal Computers arrived because people started using Computers for almost everything, then, when more snazzy and sleek and more comfortable to use Laptops were invented the demand hence the production of PC (personal computers) took a dip, than came more modern and much simpler Smartphones and Tablet Computers embedded with smart-software and more sophisticated and business friendly "Cloud Computing technology application," which has to an extent considerably reduce the demand for both PC's and laptops, once Nokia and Motorola had almost total control of mobile phone market in the world, in the 1990s Nokia was an undisputed king in mobile phone market almost everyone who use to have Cellular (mobile) phone connection in the 1990s had Nokia handset, but, when newly innovated technological products arrived in market like the Samsung's Smartphones and Apple Computers "I-pad and I-phone's," the once market leader Nokia literally got driven out of business.

Smartphones are multipurpose electronic devices, extremely user friendly and truly value for money, as Smartphones have many features and most important feature is that it has inbuilt digital Camera and Camcorder (video camera), hence smartphones can so conveniently be used for capturing live images both Still-Photography as well using camcorder helps us take Motion pictures, so all this means, substantially lower demand for more conventional Cameras and Camcorders, and with modern photography procedures having become almost fully digital, therefore demand for more traditional Colour Film rolls almost decimated. This is how businesses are put out of business. Now, this is why, it is so important for corporates to do thorough homework and in-depth analysis before they start or expand their commercial manufacturing facilities, because innovation and advancement of new technology can at any moment drive them out of business.

Sharp drop in industrial commodities prices at times also becomes a critical factor, sharp drop in prices of petroleum crude oil & gas and other industrial commodities like copper, zinc and iron-ore etc negatively impacts the manufacturing sector because the countries and companies which produces the commodities (minerals, oil & gas) earns less money hence they have less money for expenditure, which results in drop in demand for manufactured goods and products. So this is precisely the reason that corporates particularly the large Multinational companies do not necessarily bother, as in, how investor and business friendly is any particular country's business and industrial policies, they (multinational) will come to your country with tonnes of money and invest even if you don't invite them provided they see market opportunity in your country.

Don't do what others do or are doing, here I'm referring to those people who have this bizarre tendency of getting tempted into doing things what others are doing, irrational thinking, when people will see or find out that certain individuals are making big amount of money in particular business or trading a particular item which apparently is in big demand, some people in desperation gets excited and will want to do the same business as well, thinking, that they as we will be fortunate and make money, for example; "if in a particular country in a particular season if **Onion Crop** has failed which apparently has caused acute demand supply gap, due to failure of Onion crop and rising demand from consumers for Onions and because of shortage of Onion supplies (stock) has caused sharp increase in prices of Onions, few fortunate farmers and wholesalers who had physical-stocks of Onions hoarded or stored gets golden opportunity to earn big money simply by taking advantage of higher demand for Onions and rising prices of onions, now what happens is that those wholesalers and farmers who observed certain farmers who had adequate Onion stock make incredibly huge profit because of unprecedented price increase of the agri-commodity (onions), hence for the coming next season the farmers who otherwise grows Potato, tomato or garlic crop will see compelling reasons to discontinue what he has been growing all this while and instead will passionately opt to grow Onions, here, what happens is? That, because in previous season due to failed Onion crop caused short supply of onions which seemingly resulted in price of onions rise up sharply, for the next season more and more farmers thought it will be prudent for them to grow onions because of higher prices of onions in the market, so, more farmers grows onions and the crop grows successfully, that means there is more onion production, this is where the problems starts for farmers, because of increase production of onions the supply of onions increases in the market hence prices of onions drops sharply lower because of glut, huge quantity of onions becomes available in the market, meaning supply exceeds demand, drop in prices means lower cash realization for the farmers who grew onion crop, which also means most or almost all the farmers suffers huge financial loses."

Always stick to your strength, keep doing what you are best at doing, to continue with same topic further I would like to discuss about boom and bust in international commodities markets. In modern times crude petroleum oil is arguably the most significant and relevant commodity to all of mankind. Petroleum crude oil prices had risen higher sharply and dramatically in beginning of the year 2011, from U.S\$65- per barrel to a high of U.S\$120- per barrel, when crude oil prices increased sharply higher, it was all but expected that most of the countries who have large reserves of crude oil and corporates who are in the business of oil & gas exploration would get entice and increase production to sell more oil obviously to make more money, but also few countries who had until the sharp increase of oil prices had not explored their own oil reserves, they as well started working overtime to discover crude oil lying idle in their backyard spending massive amount of money trying to discover Oil fields, some countries used new age modern technology called Fracking to produce "Shale Oil," many automobile companies spent millions of dollars to develop technology to manufacture Cars that runs on alternate fuel or cars which are more fuel efficient (I would like to point out that more fuel efficient cars and cars powered by batteries are more expensive and cost lot more than compare to cars manufactured using conventional simple technology), few companies around the world also setup manufacturing units to manufacture alternate Biofuel to substitute it for more expensive fossil fuel oil. Sharp increase in crude oil prices that moved higher in 2011 remained at higher elevated level until middle of 2014, one day the inevitable happened, what goes up also has to come down, sometime in July-2014 the international commodity market busted, crude oil prices suffered major setback, the prices of Oil fell from the average higher level of U.S$110 per barrel to as low as U.S$45 per barrel in August-2015 and all this happen in matter of few months, obviously monumental decline in prices fossil fuel particularly of crude oil & gas and other industrial commodities like iron-ore, zinc, coal and copper etc jolted the entire corporate sector and even harder hit are/were prominent commodities exporting countries.

Something similar happened, when few individuals taking advantage of internet technological revolution took plunge into E-commerce business, selling products and services online or to say they became online retailers, some of the successful E-commerce ventures are "amazon.com, ebay, Alibaba.com, India's biggest online retailer Flibkart, the remarkable success of many large E-commerce companies encouraged many more new generation aspirational young men and women as well to become entrepreneur, so with high hopes many fresher's among them most with little or no work experience as well launched their own portal and website starting online retailing and offering different kinds and types of consulting services and selling products etc, seeing few people gaining and succeeding many other fence sitters ambitious youngsters sought to strengthen their career prospect and have/had jumped on the already crowded bandwagon with fair degree of optimism, and have started e-commerce business thinking that it is as easy to strive and thrive, and they as well will become rich and famous like "Jeff Bezos founder of amazon.com and Jack Ma founder of Alibaba.com," I myself am of a firm belief that e-commerce has a long way to go and those entrenched companies and formidable market players in the field of online retailing and services will see the best of times ahead and will have many glorious moments to celebrate their success and achievements, but, what happens is? When too many folks decides to become eager players and enters the ring to play the same game it spoils the party, every business and professions have its limit, no businesses or professions can accommodate more than it has capacity to absorb, it will be better advised that unless a person is convince with himself/herself that they have radically different business plan module as compare to already existing players and have extraordinary business ideas that will help them succeed and outwit potential rivals in their game plan, so, if you are certain of success only than enter the business else have no illusion and don't daydream don't enter the business which is already crowded because your entry will only add to the crowd, enter the business and professions where you see there is enough capacity left to accommodate you.

One thing that everyone must do which most people are reluctant doing, which is asking **Questions** (here what I mean is not questions regarding anyone's personal life and private affairs) regarding and related to "Business & finances, science and technology" especially at place where they work, to gain business process knowledge and to gain understanding from many different perspective to understand how different business system works, what are the policy guidelines etc, No matter at what level a person works in his/her company, whether they work as subordinate or at managerial level, it doesn't matter if they work in Steel, cement, textile manufacturing industry or in hotel, restaurant or film production company. **It doesn't cost any money to ask questions**, so, why not? ask as many questions as possible to gain comprehensive Business process and administrative knowledge, don't think on the line that it is not your business to understand others business, but try finding out more things and gather more information, as in, how things work in various business departments, back-office or on factory floor or out in the open field? How the business module is developed and planned? How the company promotes its brand and achieve sales targets? How company generates revenue and makes profits from their business operations?

Why and how asking more questions helps us in life? Because the more formal and informal discussions a person will have and ask questions to get answers and explanation from subject matter experts, it will immensely enhance the knowledge and understanding with regards to the style and manner in which businesses operates and functions, knowledge and understanding will substantially boost confidence of a person, which will eventually help him/her in life, with enhance knowledge and understanding of business process, it could possibly result in the same person who use to work as a subordinate may get promoted to higher rank in his/her office and may obtain high position in the same factory or office where a person may perhaps once had work as junior subordinate employee, or with superior knowledge and ideas of business a person will have enough confidence to start his/her own business. This is one of the principal formula of success, using this very formula few smart individuals have risen from Rags to Riches.

Don't downgrade your dreams just to fit your reality, upgrade your conviction to make your destiny.

Few of the prominent countries like to play it easy and banks profoundly on the available natural resources like Crude Oil or other Minerals, few notable examples are, **Chile** a south-American country is overwhelmingly and comprehensively dependant on its Copper reserves, Chile's fortunes are intrinsically linked to the price movement of Copper, because it has large reserves of Copper deposits hidden under its surface, another south-American country **Venezuela** which is also a prime example, Venezuela has enormous reserves of petroleum Crude Oil, hence the country and its citizens for years and decades have been relying resolutely on single source of revenue, which it earns from selling petroleum Oil in the international markets. Each country needs to have a balanced economic system and business diversity with fully integrated industrial units which sources the raw materials and adds higher value to the products they manufacture, to get better price realizations in the markets.

If Mistakes have been Committed, so, Learn from the Past Mistakes and Have it Correct the Next time.

"Create economic value and do not destroy economic value, higher profits and value is in value addition. Do not give away advantage, learn to make optimal use of the resources you have for your own benefits. Efficient resource management is extremely important to increase productivity, which will immensely help increase profit margins."

When prices of commodities falls sharply, many businesses suffers unbelievable loses, many governments particularly those of commodity producing countries feels extreme pain, just to name a few, large mineral mining companies like BHP Billiton and Rio Tinto or the big Oil exploration and producing companies like Exxon Mobil, British Petroleum and Chevron Corporation, as all these large and many more companies in similar business also Brokers and Traders of commodities their fortunes are largely dependent on the market prices of various hard commodity, when prices of commodities are declining obviously the companies in the business of mining and oil exploration feels extreme pressure on their Balance Sheets and suffers extreme pain of declining profitability from their business operations.

Countries for example Iraq and Venezuela, Russia and Norway or Brazil and Australia, all suffers extremely hard due to the steep fall in prices of various commodities which each of these countries produce and trade in, particularly hard hit are nations like Iraq and Venezuela because these two countries fortunes immensely depends on the price of crude oil in international markets, so if the crude oil prices trade at or below U.S$50/52 per barrel in which case the Iraqi and Venezuela governments will have little or No money to spend on social sector, public welfare schemes and programmes, thus will have to cut spending which means more hardship to already distressful citizens of Iraq and Venezuela.

Not just financial and stock-markets but even currency markets feels the pressure, currency markets around the world experiences brutal volatility and currency dealers feels the jitters, during times when commodity markets are unstable and prices of commodities are stumbling, for example if prices of iron-ore, gold, coking coal or oil & gas drops, commodity producing countries like Australia, Russia, Nigeria, Brazil and South-Africa will earn lot less foreign exchange, seeing such countries economy in trouble, canny investors would like to move their money out of these beleaguered countries and move it (money) to other safe destination, hence in uncertain times the overseas astute investors will try to unload debt instruments and liquidate assets and capital investments from such economically weaker nations, what adds to the woes is that, less foreign exchange comes in and more foreign exchange goes out of the country. In 2013 approximate currency value of One Aussie Dollar use to buy U.S$ 0.95, and in September-2015 One Aussie Dollar could buy only U.S$0.70, similarly Russian Ruble as well suffered severe losses against major international currencies like U.S dollar and European Euro, in 2013 approximately Russian Ruble 38 or 40 were required to buy One U.S dollar and in September-2015 Ruble got massively devalued and Russian Ruble 68 needed to buy One U.S dollar.

Banks, Asset management companies, Financial institutions and High Net-worth investors no matter where they are based whether in U.S or Europe, Singapore or

Hong Kong, when Banks and fund managers makes strategic investment in countries like Russia, Australia, Brazil and South-Africa by taking large exposure in Stock Markets of these countries by buying Shares of companies and also investing in corporate debt and buying large quantity of Government backed Securities & Bonds, such investments are considered as high risk high return investments, if these banks and financial institutions "Asset management team/fund managers" are clever, they will appropriately time the market's volatility and move out of the market as soon as they see trouble brewing, as in financial market you may have heard this financial jargon, which says "**buy low and sell high**," smart money "buys low and sells high," fool's money will "buy high and sell low."

Sharp volatility in resource (commodities) prices makes resource rich countries economy more unstable, what adds to the problem is the role of strategic investors, international banks and investors **rush in** to invest big amount of money when commodities prices are higher, and **rush out** of the country when commodities prices are declining, abrupt flow in and flow out of large amount of foreign money, all of which causes instability in both stock-markets and currency markets, such high uncertainty about economic growth, that's precisely the reason, why you'll find much higher unemployment in most of the natural resource rich countries.

One problem creates another problem, the problems with problem is, that, they just keep adding on, if there is problem in commodity markets it will create problems in currency and stock-markets and all three problems combine together creates massive social and political problems.

Countries like Australia and Canada are well diversified economies, so they are less impacted whenever there is turmoil in commodity markets, country like Norway may feel less pain as well due to decline in Oil & gas prices because its finances are well managed and also surplus money is meticulously invested, but many other countries which are not well diversified enough and are overwhelmingly reliant and dependent on their country's natural resources for their survival will always feel extreme distress and pain, countries like Iraq, Nigeria, Venezuela and Iran which are largely dependent upon income they earn from selling petroleum oil, country like Chile which so heavily depends on the money it earns from its Copper production and trade, or South Africa which earns enormous amount of money selling Gold, Platinum and other minerals.

Countries like China, India, South Korea, Italy and many other European and American countries economy will get negatively impacted when there is turmoil in commodity markets, that's because the Iraqis, Iranians, Russians and Brazilians besides also many citizens from Saudi Arabia, Australia and Canada will have less money to spend on Bling and also on many other essential consumer items as well, because they earn lot less money therefore governments of large commodity producing and trading countries will cut spending, people from Russia, Brazil and Australia will avoid travelling to foreign countries to spend holidays, in which case countries which are mainstream tourist destinations will suffer and feel downward pressure on their own economies. Spending power of citizens of large commodity producing countries will significantly diminish due to profound fall in prices of the natural resources they own and also because of sharp depreciation (devaluation) of their respective countries currency, so they will buy less products from countries like China, Korea, Italy and India etc, therefore exports and tourism industry in most countries will suffer and feel intense recessionary pressures because of depressing demand for manufactured products, consumer discretionary products and other items of day to day consumptions. Substantial drop in demand due to consumer spending cuts will particularly slow down manufacturing sector in China and South-Korea.

Lower demand from overseas customers for its products will considerably slow down Chinese export growth which in turn will immensely harm China's manufacturing sector, if Chinese manufacturing sector is in bad-health, than obviously the factory and industry owners will reduce their workforce, if people in China are without work and are jobless then it will lower the purchasing power of Chinese folks, hence, Chinese domestic consumer demand will recedes, which in turn will further deteriorate Chinese manufacturing sector and potentially cause more job losses in Chinese manufacturing sector, all these negative factors means, China's import will register drastic cut, yes, if Chinese exports are not increasing plus purchasing power of China's citizens is ebbing, in that case China will import lot less products from overseas, this is where things will take an ugly turn, call it Chinese effect, if you want to, but slowing Chinese economic growth will decelerate entire world's economic growth and will cause brutal global economic recession. So, agree or disagree but it is true, China is the most sought after and most relevant country in the world. What makes China and Chinese so important for the rest of the world? Perhaps the answer would be, the sheer size of the country's population, it seems for China its large population of nearly 1.4-Billion people is its biggest asset.

Otherwise there is a famous saying "**the less the better**" but, No, with regards to China and India the saying would be "**the more the better**" for both China and India, what matters most is there huge Population.

Commodity is a cyclical business, commodities prices will keep moving up and down depending on demand and supply. But there is another perspective and a much bigger perspective for us to understand, as in, how much really the natural resource rich countries have gained all these years and decades by selling whatever minerals and petroleum oil & gas reserves their countries have? We all know how rich and wealthy the Arabs and Russians became by selling petroleum oil & gas to international buyers also not left behind are many more countries and there citizens who all have amass huge wealth like the Norwegians, Canadians and Australians all in the business of trading in petroleum oil & gas and many other strategic mineral reserves that are abundantly available and hidden in their respective countries land. "But and a big "**But,**" have these supreme Natural Resources Rich nations, have they actually made enough money as much as potentially they could have or had by selling and exporting Oil and Minerals? Or, have they lost out on something even bigger? A more thorough deep check will prove, they've missed or still are missing opportunity to earn much more **money** than they are actually earning. Than another bigger question arises; Have these natural resources rich countries politicians and economic policies makers and advisors really goofed-up big time and therefore inadvertently denied and deprived their countries larger population from potentially earning millions of dollars and becoming Millionaires and Billionaires?

Let's find out.

Natural resources are material and substances that are provided to humans by Earth, for which we humans have developed technic and technologies to exploit it for our commercial gain and personal interest, Natural resources are useful raw material made available to us (humans) by Earth to make more complex products from it for our consumption. But as we humans have divided our Planet Earth into many different zones, regions and countries, therefore in this bigger planet Not every country is fortunate to have vast reserves and deposits of minerals and petroleum oil & gas, there are only few countries, in total maybe 25 to 30 countries which have been fortunate to have extremely large quantities of crude oil & gas or many other different types of strategic mineral reserves, also some countries have extremely fertile land which is most suitable for agriculture production, while many countries do not have suitable weather condition or for some other reasons their Land is less fertile hence No or very little cultivatable land for Agri farming.

Few names of prominent countries which have large reserves and deposits of Oil & gas and minerals are Australia, Canada, Brazil, Russia, Saudi Arabia and Iran etc, these countries makes extensive use of available natural resources for commercial purpose and exploit it for economic gains, they sell to international buyers or to say exports minerals like copper, iron-ore, coal, bauxite, gold, zinc and many other different types of minerals. Russians, Saudis and Iranians are predominantly large players in energy business, these countries exports crude oil and natural gas. The major consuming nations like China, Japan, European countries, South Korea, India and many more countries buy supplies of Oil & gas and other minerals like iron-ore, zinc and copper etc, the importing countries then Refines Crude oil and makes value added products like Petrol, Diesel and cooking gas and many other speciality chemicals and plastic products that are made from crude oil & gas in large Refineries and Petro-chemical complex, also minerals like raw iron-ore is use to make Iron & Steel and other value added products from Steel in countries like China, Korea and Japan.

Now this is interesting to note, where and how these natural resource rich nations are goofing up big time, and, how? Have a listen, a country like Australia exports iron-ore and even coking coal (metallurgical coal) to overseas buyers for example to countries like "China and South Korea," The Iron & Steel companies in China and Korea adds value to iron-ore and coking-coal to produce raw Iron and Steel and further adds value to raw Iron and Steel by making more productive high value-added products from Iron and Steel which they then sell it to various user industries like construction and automobiles manufacturers. Similarly Russia exports large quantity of Oil & Gas to European countries where the domestic refineries and petro-chemical companies uses Russian oil and gas to make many different types of value added products like Auto fuel, cooking gas, heating oil, speciality chemicals etc. what more? The refined value-added petro-chemical products are sold domestically in European markets and also large quantity is exported to many other countries, interestingly many high value-added petro-chemical products are also exported to Russia as well to many Arab countries, same countries from where raw crude oil and gas is sourced.

Now suppose if a family have a "**Hen that lays Golden Egg**" every day, so, what does the family members who are the most fortunate to have a Hen which provides a Golden Egg everyday do with the availability of free precious Gold? The head of that family goes to the jewellery market every day and sells the Golden egg, returns back home every day with loads of cash in his pocket and with easy cash (money) derived from selling gold which apparently is available for free, thus, the family enjoys and cherishes every moment of their life. Now; How about the family members decides upon not to sell the Golden egg every day in the jewellery market, but instead decides to melt the golden egg and on daily basis uses the gold which their Hen is providing them to make more productive use of the available resources (Gold) to add higher value to it, and starts making designer gold ornaments, hires professional Artisans to design jewellery and to manufacture ornaments from gold, creates a Brand and then Sells the staggeringly attractive Branded products which are the specially designed gold ornaments in the open market to the customers, now see the difference, what happens? The family earlier conveniently without any effort use to receive cash in hand by selling their golden egg in raw form and use to sit idle the whole day doing nothing, simply spending money on eating and drinking, buying expensive clothes and afford many more luxuries of life, all with the money they use to get from selling the golden egg, but later they became active and started using the golden egg to add value to it by making fashionable designer jewellery and gold ornaments, therefore the family became physically active and interactive also became more creative and innovative and started working hard, and guess, what? They started earning much more money than they use to earn before when they use to sell precious golden egg in raw form to the jeweller. From richness the family became wealthy and more worthwhile because the family started utilizing its resources which was free availability of gold to create high yielding branded jewellery products, the designer jewellery and gold ornaments.

Value addition gives much higher and better returns, so in real terms the countries which have large reserves of minerals, petroleum oil and gas, for them the natural resources is like a family silver, you inherit family wealth and silver, then it's your responsibility to add value and create more wealth from it, simply "**Selling family Silver to pay the Butler**" is not a good proposition and most inappropriate manner of utilizing family Wealth. This is precisely what most or almost every nation which are rich in natural resources are doing, simply mining (digging into the earth) and extracting minerals loading the minerals on the cargo ships and exporting it to the foreign buyers, same way the oil and gas is being pumped out from the Oil Wells and poured in the empty barrels and loaded in ships and exporting it to foreign countries, the countries that imports petroleum oil & gas and other minerals in raw form they then supply imported materials to the Refineries, petro-chemical industries and Factories based in their countries where the oil and minerals are refined and processed and then productively used for making thousands of different types of value added products which are then sold in the open markets to the end users and consumers at steep premium which could potentially be 4 to 8 times higher price as compare to the original cost-price at which they had purchased the basic raw material, therefore scoring spectacular profitable points.

Do a strict reality check and we'll find that Britain in 18th an 19th century had spectacularly utilized domestically available natural resources to begin and to power the Industrial revolution, British made excellent use of available natural resources like Coal, iron-ore and many other minerals to Industrialized their nation and to spur optimal economic growth, not only Britain did it, but the entire Europe made extensive and comprehensive use of locally available natural resources to power economic growth which helped create jobs and business opportunities. Britain used domestically available Thermal-coal to generate electricity and used iron-ore and coal to manufacture iron and steel and many other value added products, Britain also pioneer itself in textile business, many woollen mills were started in Britain in 18th and 19th century, using its own natural resources to produce goods in their own country; mining, textile, steel and power generating companies created hundreds of thousands of jobs and business opportunities in Britain.

Another great country "United States of America" as well made magnificent use of domestically available natural resources when in 19th century it started its own Industrial and Transport revolution, manufacturing facilities were created in U.S. and domestically available natural resources were meticulously and constructively used as feedstock and raw materials to manufacture industrial and household consumer products. Another large nation China as well has been using its own natural resources as raw material to manufacture many different types of industrial and consumer products. This are three exemplary examples of prominent countries (Britain, U.S. China), how instead of selling natural resources such as minerals, oil & gas and agriculture commodities **raw and cheap** to overseas buyers they made enhance use of available natural resources, used minerals, oil & gas and agriculture commodities to manufacture industrial and consumer products and to generate power (electricity), thereby these ambitious great countries created jobs and also provided many of their citizens great quality and quantitative opportunities to earn big-money and become millionaires.

Selling family silver for survival, does it make sense? Whether we talk of an individual person or a country, selling personal assets or liquidating wealth (gold, silver or properties etc) for cash can potentially make a person or a country rich but they won't be considered worthwhile or wealthy. Large exporting countries of petroleum crude oil & gas and other strategic industrial commodities and minerals, countries for example: Russia, Saudi Arabia, Canada, Brazil and many other smaller nations particularly from Africa needs to learn to use their initiative, imagination and common sense.

Consuming nations which imports Crude oil & gas, and minerals like copper, iron-ore, metallurgical coal, bauxite and zinc etc, gains immensely, India, China, Thailand, European nations and many more countries buys crude oil at much lower price and then the standalone petroleum refineries in their country Refines crude oil to make high value added products like Gasoline (petrol), diesel, aviation turbine fuel (jet fuel) and many more petroleum products, textiles, plastics and chemicals and then sells it in open market to customers for incredibly higher amount, similarly with minerals like iron-ore, copper, bauxite and zinc are used extensively and resolutely to produce high quality Iron and Steel products, further value is added by making more productive items like Electrical cables, wires, pipes, iron rods and so many more consumer items and then sold to end users for higher value.

Now suppose country like Australia which has large deposits and reserves of many different kinds of minerals and fossil fuels, if country like Australia utilizes its entire iron-ore and metallurgical coal (coking coal) production domestically, by setting up large Industrial units to manufacture Iron and Steel and further make more value added iron and steel products and then exports it to consumers in foreign countries, same if Australians uses entire bauxite capacity to manufacture Aluminium in their own country and then exports it to foreign countries, similarly uses Coal to manufacture value added products and then export it. Following similar pattern if other large commodity producing countries like Russia, Brazil, Canada and many other African nations who have large reserves of natural resources sets up large manufacturing capacities in their own country and then exports semi-finished or finished value-added products as per demand from buyers in foreign countries, if these countries makes absolute commercial use of the entire domestically available natural resources themselves by setting up large manufacturing facilities in their own country, in which case countries like Australia, Canada, Brazil, Iraq, Nigeria, South-Africa would be creating millions of jobs and create more lucrative business opportunities for their own nationals, manufacturing and production of industrial products increases country's trade and commerce and creates more and more business opportunities, thereby opening up opportunities for millions of their own citizens to obtain wealth if they have relevant talent and skills, suitable commercial utilization of naturally available natural resources helps more individuals of your own country to become millionaires.

As we do deep research, we discover it's a **Three Hundred Trillion Dollar goof up**, since 1960s and 70s many large petroleum Oil & gas producing countries have been exporting millions of barrels of petroleum oil per day in raw/crude form, Russia and Saudi Arabia are the two biggest producers and exporters of crude oil, each of these two countries exports over 9 million barrels of crude oil every day, other prominent crude oil exporting countries are Iraq, Norway, Nigeria,

Venezuela and Iran, plus there are other nations like Kazakhstan and Angola which as well have emerged as significant players in petroleum oil production, so, for years these large petroleum exporting countries have been exporting crude oil in raw form, unprocessed and unrefined.

Now instead of exporting their most invaluable and irreplaceable wealth "**Crude oil**" in raw unrefined form, suppose if countries like Russia, Iraq, Nigeria, Venezuela and Saudi Arabia would have set-up large petroleum refineries in their own respective country for the purpose of refining their entire crude oil output, and if these countries were to have started a mega big petrochemical plants and factories in their own country to manufacture highly complex and distinctly productive petrochemical and chemical products using vast domestically available crude oil as raw-material to manufacture products like "Asphalt, paraffin wax, petroleum coke, lubricating oil and grease, purified terephthalic acid" and many more such petroleum products, and also countries like Saudi Arabia, Iraq and Russia taking advantage of domestically available crude oil could have more productively used it to manufacture refining products like Auto fuel, jet fuel, LPG gas (propane gas) in refineries based in their own countries, so if the Russians, Saudis, Iraqis, Nigerians and Iranians all large producers of petroleum crude oil, instead of selling their crude oil so crudely to overseas buyers, had these countries governments would have used better imagination and set-up large Oil Refineries in their respective country and also set-up large petrochemical complex and would have effectively used those facilities to refine petroleum oil and to manufacture value-added petrochemical products and then should have exported, or in more simple terms instead of selling crude oil in crude form, all these years and decades, if petroleum crude oil producing countries would have manufactured petroleum products in their own country and then exported finish petroleum products to the end buyers/consumers overseas or sold it domestically to home consumers/customers, can anyone imagine how much more money these oil producing countries would have earned.

There are countries like Russia, Qatar and Norway which are large exporters of natural gas, Iran as well have massive reserves of natural gas, similarly like crude oil even **Natural Gas** is a viable raw material to produce many higher value added products, natural gas is used for many different purposes, one of the main use is to generate electricity, Natural gas is a key raw material to manufacture highly lucrative petrochemical products, like "Ethylene, polymers, ammonia and many other types of complex chemicals and fertilizer products," in addition also auto fuel can be made from natural gas. For adding better **Economic-value**, if large natural gas producing countries like Russia, Norway, Qatar and Iran sets up large Gas cracker industries in their respective country to manufacture products like ethylene and polymers which finds extensive usage in producing high quality plastic materials, footwear, plus ethylene and polymers are basic raw material for manufacturing many engineering and electronic products. So, setting up manufacturing facilities to make superlative use of available natural resources by adding further value and then selling it either in domestic markets or exporting it to foreign countries, it makes sense, wherever possible creating and adding more value to the product is always going to be more profitable and will create more wealth for the companies as well for countries. More so, having manufacturing facilities helps citizens of the country learn new skills, helps in gaining better knowledge and understanding about business processes and technologies, importantly it gives citizens better sense of satisfaction as they feel that they as well are playing significant role in the development of their country.

"Countries, particularly the countries with massive natural resources needs to learn to create high quality Economic-value and Not to destroy Economic-value."

Almost all these large petroleum crude oil & gas producing and exporting countries are losing big time big money, just imagine if countries like Russia, Saudi Arabia, Nigeria, Venezuela, Norway etc would have set-up mega large Refining capacities and petrochemical projects for extensive commercial use of their entire **Crude oil and gas output** to refine and to manufacture fuel oil and petrochemical products both for domestic consumption and for exports to foreign countries, these countries would have created so much additional wealth for themselves and for their citizens, **almost every family in Saudi, Russia, Iran, Iraq would have become worth millions of U.S.-dollars.**

Whatever the business and profession you are in, whether its petroleum oil and gas, metals and minerals, or dairy and agriculture products, cocoa beans, potatoes, oranges or milk, every product will provide better and higher cash-margins and yields once you add value to it, use raw potatoes to make potato chips, cheese-potato patties or hot fry potatoes it will sell at much higher than anticipated price, use crude oil & gas to make auto-fuel and petrochemical products the yields will be phenomenon, use milk to make ice-creams, branded yogurts or milkshakes unprecedented profits will be made, using Wheat grain to manufacture biscuits or artisan breads it provides excellent profits. So, whether we talk about countries, companies or individuals, you always need to be creative and keep thinking something new and productive, be astute, never give others competitive advantage, look for what's going to be a better deal for you, **in business and trade "Not Emotions" but Profitability is what matters most**.

Whenever the topic of discussion is about Economic backwardness, social injustice, poverty, malnutrition and many other human problems, one region and a significant part of the world is particularly mentioned and discussed, that region is a continent called **Africa**. I've heard many intellectuals and academicians saying that Africa is a **Rich Continent** but with lots of Poor People staying in Africa, yes I agree, and most experts and analysts are of the view that the main reason for all round backwardness and plight of most people in Africa who are deprived of many basic human needs, they blame Social, religious and political tension which seemingly causes social unrest and political turmoil and instability in most of African countries, but, more importantly it halts economic progress and development.

Social and Political scientist and experts each of them will highlight different reasons behind the backwardness and extreme poverty in Africa, but, who is to be blame? Why for generations the Africans have remained economically backwards? Despite the fact, a genuine fact that Africa has everything gifted to it by Nature that one would ask to have, it has large reserves of minerals, fossil fuels and many parts of Africa have most suitable and cultivable agricultural farming-land. According to my own assessments, the reason for sharp social and economic backwardness in Africa is, entire Africa's flawed Business and Economic policies.

Many different types of minerals can be found in Africa in abundance, natural resources particularly minerals like copper, iron-ore and manganese then large reserves of Coal, Gold and Diamonds and specially the most lucrative of all agriculture commodity, that's, "**Cocoa beans**."

In the western parts of Africa there are several countries that grows large quantity of Cocoa beans, and in south and central Africa there are several countries which have large reserves of minerals, Diamonds are one among many prominently available precious gemstones in south and central African region.

West-African countries like Ivory Coast (also known as "Cote d'Ivoire) and Ghana between them accounts for according to some estimates nearly 55% of world's Cocoa Beans market, Cocoa-beans is the most precious and prestigious agriculture commodity, many fabulously delicious food and eating items and products are made with cocoa being its main ingredient, almost everyone in the world likes to eat various different kinds of products that are made from cocoa, whether its Chocolates, biscuits, cakes, ice-creams. What's worth noting is that each of the prominent cocoa-beans producing countries in Africa be it "Ivory Coast, Ghana, Nigeria and Cameroon," each of these large cocoa beans producing countries keeps very little of their cocoa beans produce for their own domestic consumption and for more high-yielding commercial usage but Exports almost entire production of cocoa beans in raw form to many different parts of the world. In Europe, America or Asia there are thousands of companies in organized and unorganised sector which uses cocoa beans as principle raw material and produces many different types of high-yielding value added products for mass consumption and earns massive profits, globally annual business turnover of products and items made from cocoa beans is Hundreds of Billions of U.S. dollars.

Suppose if these prominent cocoa beans producing African countries like Ivory Coast, Ghana and Cameroon instead of exporting cocoa beans in raw form to other influential nations around the world, if making pragmatic choice, these African countries use their entire Cocoa Beans production domestically and sets up manufacturing facilities by opening factories to manufacture value added high-end products like "Chocolates, biscuits, milkshakes and cakes," and then Exports the finish products to other parts of the world, the benefits derived from value addition will be enormous, so, with more meaningful and effective use of domestically available commodity (in this case- cocoa-beans) the same Africans, most of whom, who are socially backwards and have been living in extreme poverty will begin to thrive, all they (Africans) need to do is to use little bit of common sense and high imagination.

Similar issues in case of **Diamonds** as well, there is a famous saying **"Diamonds are girl's best friend"** but it seems the Africans don't have love for the sparkling stones (diamonds) which are found right under their own feet, that's why they export almost entire diamond production unpolished (uncut), African country "Botswana" is supposed to be the 2nd largest Diamond producing country in the world, other African countries which also have considerably large Diamond production are South-Africa, Namibia and Angola, very little production of their diamonds do these countries ever Cut and Polish before selling it mainly to overseas buyers, almost entire production of diamonds are exported in **rough form** or to say without polishing and cutting diamonds in precise sizes, It will be interesting to understand that, when the diamonds are polished and cut in precise sizes that's when diamonds command higher premium prices.

India for decades is and has remain undisputed king in diamond trade, India imports approximately 70 to 80% of rough (uncut) diamonds from many different diamond producing countries, the diamonds are than Polished and Cut in appropriate sizes and then exported to major markets around the world particularly to the rich nations, thereby diamond business owners makes huge profits as they gain much higher premium, but few smart diamond merchants in India makes even better and more constructive use of the cut-diamonds by using it to make stylish diamond jewellery and then either sells diamond-jewellery in domestic markets or exports trendy and fashionable diamond jewellery which yields exceedingly higher profits for the Indian diamond merchants and traders. Diamond merchants and traders are the most affluent business community in India because they have stupendous money power hence they have exceptionally high spending power.

Whether we talk about or analyse business and trade policies of diamond producing nations or "cocoa beans, iron-ore, coal, petroleum oil or copper" producing nations, if countries with large reserves of natural resources would continue to sell their produce in raw and crude form, and will not bother to achieve better economies of scale by "forward or vertically integrating" their business operations by using domestically available raw materials to make productive use of it and to make and produce high-end value added products which are manufactured in their own country's factories and industrial units and then sold either in home markets or foreign markets. When there are no factories and manufacturing industrial units in their own country, the citizens of that country feels deprived as they do not get opportunity to manifest their creative abilities and do not get a chance to learn new business processes. When significantly large population of a particular country isn't getting a chance and opportunity to learn new skills and or in extreme circumstances is/are systematically being denied or deprived of professional opportunities, that is what creates a situation, when some citizens starts feeling discomfort with their country's system and starts thinking that they are being discriminated, hence in frustration vulnerable individuals makes irrational choices and takes rash decisions and recklessly adopts unconventional means and toxic methods of living life.

The inequality between rich and poor nations is getting wider, rising income inequality in both developed and under-developed countries, widening gap between rich and poor, rich people becoming more rich and poor are becoming more poor, bi-polar division between affluent class and underclass, has become acute intractable global problem, because, chronic poverty not only harms those countries affected by it but it threatens the entire world's peace and stability.

Some of the principle natural resources rich nations needs to do some serious rethinking with regards to their countries economic and trade policies, understand the significance of value-addition and relevance of using naturally available resources as raw material to produce high-end value-added products by setting up manufacturing facilities in their own country. Natural resources rich countries needs to take quick radical measures and steps to rework and redraft their country's business and trade policies, as things stands for now, they are decisively losing advantage and are serving incredibly steep monetary benefits on the platter in the most simplest of manner, providing ample opportunities to the outsiders to make Billions and Trillions of dollars. Never stick to a single business strategy always good to have multiple business strategies.

In real life to deal with real life issues, a person needs to be Street-Smart, the most pragmatic assessment of real life realities proves that being Street-smart counts more than any other kinds of smartness/intelligence.

Success and failures are part of everyone's life, hence there is no harm in trying and failing in your attempt to achieve your goals and objectives in life, rather than, **Not** trying to achieve your goals and objectives in life, because assuming and pre-empting fearful thoughts and feelings in your mind, thinking that you will again fail in your endeavour, there is no shame in failing. We must graciously learn to accept our failures. So, don't allow few chaotic incidents to halt your progress, don't fear, instead, remove all obstacles that are in the way preventing you from succeeding in life.

Don't be too hard on yourself. There are plenty of people willing to do that for you. Love yourself and be proud of everything you do, Even mistakes mean you are trying.

Is being greedy good or bad? This perhaps is one of the most controversial question, for years academicians and scholars have been debating to understand "Is it good or bad for we humans to be greedy?" how I would prefer to describe is, that, greed has two side of it, on positive side, greed makes us (humans) more result oriented, more productive, challenges us to become more creative and innovative, greed makes us more disciplined so that we love and take care of our near and dear ones and that we maintain hygiene and keep environment and surrounding clean.

The negative repercussions of Greed, on negative side, Greed is self-destructive and devastatingly bad, greed can have unimaginable consequences. Greedy people are callous in their manoeuvres, they are manipulative and destructive elements.

Greed is a catalyst for most of human's problems and real reason behind many perpetrated crimes as well for corruption and violence around the world, there are millions of millionaires and billionaires in our world, among millions of millionaires there are also many who have accumulated wealth by unfair and corrupt means.

Greed makes a person corrupt and callous, for some people their only objective in life is to accumulate personal wealth by any means possible, to accumulate wealth and to become rich some people can go to any extent, they don't mind selling adulterated products, counterfeit currency-notes, counterfeit medicines without bothering about the consequences and devastating impact it will have on common people who will consume it, those people in sleazy trade of selling and trading in counterfeit medicines and adulterated food items do it without any remorse, such people are ruthless.

Domestic violence is a bigger menace than compare to terrorism or conventional military wars, yes, surprising, but this is what many research surveys and studies conducted by many human rights and civil rights groups have found out that domestic violence is much more devastatingly harmful, troublesome and cost-wise as well very expensive than compare to terrorism or wars fought by military in the battlefields.

The menace of Domestic Violence occurred since the civilized life came into existence on this planet (Earth), Violence against women is a manifestation of unequal physical-power equation between men and women. Domestic Violence occurs as a repercussion of temperamental and behavioural-problems, poverty, social backwardness, and centuries old baseless cultural traditions. Rigidly defined roles for women in many conservative societies. Behind closed doors of homes all across the world people are being tortured, beaten and killed. Victim of domestic violence suffers extreme mental stress and surge in anxiety, so, domestic violence and workplace violence are devastatingly traumatizing, victims of domestic violence or intimate relationship violence are unable to concentrate or focus on their work, therefore the effects of domestic violence can destroy professional careers.

Difficult people will always create difficult situations, at home or at workplace or for that matter even in social circle, "it will be better not to try and **reason** the **unreasonable** person," so, you need to have the right **temperament** to remain calm in pressure situation.

Have a assertive and positive approach, differences and contentious issues needs to be sorted out amicably through dialogue and cordial discussions, one very important lesson to learn in life is, never to **Argue**, *argument is worst form of violence*, arguments normally have devastating consequences, arguments destroys personal image and gives bad reputation, arguments strains relationships or even causes breakup of relationships, be it in personal life, professional or business life, also frequent arguments precipitates <u>domestic violence</u> as well <u>workplace violence</u>, so be better advised, **always avoid argument**.

Common Sense is like a Deodorant, The People who needs it most Never use it.

<u>Fickle minded person</u>, are people with such a characteristic, *they don't know what they want in life*, hesitation and full of confusion, such people not only do they disrupt their own progress, but they also harm and halt progress of others as well, and always a spoilsport will ruin other people's peace. In stark contrast a person who has **self-confidence** and strong **body-language** will always attract attention of people wherever he/she goes, people in our society always like, respect, believe and trust a person who is self-confident, experts are of the opinion that self-confidence is first step towards Progress and development so as to achieve success in life.

We all have expectations in our lives, what we want out of life and what we want to become in life, managing our expectations, the problem arise in a person's life when their expectations do not materialize, most people especially educated folks goof up bigtime in life, because they are unaware of basic ground realities. Schools and universities text books makes a person book-smart what counts more in real life is to be **street-smart**.

Have your own perspective and challenge your perspective, which will help you take appropriate decisions.

Be Positive, think, talk and behave Positively, your Positive body language and talks will help people around you feel more confident in you and they'll trust you, Positive thinking and thoughts will render positive energy to you, Positive thinking of yours will result in Positive outcomes.

In business as well in social life, what is more important is not just how good you talk, good communication skills is important, but even more important is how good and stunning is your body language, most people do not understand the significance of Body language, how you "Stand, Dress, Move, Interact, Eye contacts and Smile" it all matters the most, Body language is a kind of Non-Verbal communication between individuals, it is observed more intensely, both, consciously and unconsciously, the impact of body language far outweighs what people say and how they say it and How others Judge us and how we Judge others.

Negative thinking and thoughts will make you pessimist, talking, thinking and behaving negatively will make people around you nervous and sceptical, Negative thoughts and thinking will give sleepless nights that will also negatively impact your health, a person whose thoughts and beliefs are negative it as well results in negative outcomes.

What people need to have the most? It is to have a quality "**Analytical Skills,**" to solve complex and uncomplicated problems.

No matter how good an orator you are, how good is your communication skills and proficiency in language/languages you may have. But, what actually will save you from many troubles of life is a **Good Listening Skills**, yes, most people invites unnecessary troubles in their life as well as many family's disintegrate because of **Bad Listening Skills**. **Good Listening Skills** is a Master's Art, unfortunately most people don't know the great significance of "**Critical Listening Skills.**"

The most important kind of freedom is to be what you really are. You trade in your reality for a rate. You trade in your sense for an act. You give up your ability to feel, and in exchange, put on a mask. There can't be any large-scale revolution, on an individual level. It's got to happen inside first.

Smart person learns from his/her own mistakes, smarter/smartest person learns from others mistakes.

Keep learning new things as long as your life permits you to, never lose hope in yourself, keep all options open, there is nothing too difficult in life, all you need is to be dedicated and determined to achieve your objectives.

www.ingramcontent.com/pod-product-compliance
Lightning Source LLC
Chambersburg PA
CBHW062008280526
45787CB00005B/2015